# MA+H
## YOU CAN'T USE

# MA+H
## YOU CAN'T USE

Patents, Copyright, and Software

Ben Klemens

**Brookings Institution Press**
*Washington, D.C.*

MT

Copyright © 2006
THE BROOKINGS INSTITUTION
1775 Massachusetts Avenue, N.W., Washington, D.C. 20036
www.brookings.edu

*Library of Congress Cataloging-in-Publication data*

Klemens, Ben.
    Math you can't use : patents, copyright, and software / Ben Klemens.
        p.        cm.
    Summary: "Gathering persepectives from law, computer science, mathematics, and economics, examines the intellectual property issues surrounding computer software and suggests how patents might accommodate the unique structure of code and copyright for software could be more effectively implemented"—Provided by publisher.
    Includes bibliographical references and index.
    ISBN-13: 978-0-8157-4942-4 (cloth : alk. paper)
    ISBN-10: 0-8157-4942-2 (cloth : alk. paper)
    1. Intellectual property.   2. Intellectual property—United States.   3. Computer software—Law and legislation.   I. Title.
K1519.C6.K54 2005
346.04'8—dc22                                                              2005027332

9 8 7 6 5 4 3 2 1

The paper used in this publication meets minimum requirements of the American National Standard for Information Sciences—Permanence of Paper for Printed Library Materials: ANSI Z39.48-1992.

Typeset in Sabon

Composition by R. Lynn Rivenbark
Macon, Georgia

Printed by R. R. Donnelley
Harrisonburg, Virginia

12/28/06

# Contents

Preface                                                    vii

CHAPTER ONE
Introduction                                                 1

CHAPTER TWO
Optimal Breadth                                             12

CHAPTER THREE
From Equations to Software                                 24

CHAPTER FOUR
Patenting Math                                             44

CHAPTER FIVE
Profiting from Overbroad Patents                           73

CHAPTER SIX
The Decentralized Software Market                          92

CHAPTER SEVEN
Interoperability                                          108

CHAPTER EIGHT
Protecting Text                                           131

CHAPTER NINE
Policy Recommendations                                    151

Glossary                                                  161
References                                                167
Index                                                     171

# Preface

I am a quant. Almost all of my work involves either pure math or writing computer code to calculate numbers—even this book will rely on one mathematical theorem (which I promise will be painless). In my free time, I've done things like write a video game and a short guide to statistical analysis using the C programming language.

But this is a policy book about writing good laws, so let me summarize what I want from the law: to be left alone to write code and do math. I am not trying to rationalize or alibi theft; I just want to be able to do calculations and write programs using my own ingenuity without worrying that anyone will have a claim on my results.

I am not exactly worried that a jackbooted lawyer might kick down my door at three in the morning. I distribute little of my code to the world, and statistics is not the most lucrative of fields. But I can't write code in a vacuum and need tools written by others to do the hard parts. With increasing frequency, software projects are being shut down or crippled because of legal problems. As a result, I can do less.

When my brother bought a Linux PC so he could run simulations of new circuit designs, he asked me (his twenty-four-hour tech support hotline) how he could use the machine to listen to his music in MP3 format. "Sorry," I explained, "that would infringe patents. You'll need to purchase a copy of Windows, since Microsoft has negotiated the appropriate licenses." What about using the PC to watch the DVDs in his living room? Nope, violates federal law. Can't be done unless you want to be an outlaw and download C code from Brazil and recompile it on your PC. How about just watching QuickTime movies from the Internet? Sorry again, but QuickTime depends on the Sorensen Codec, and Sorensen won't let Linux programmers write anything that can read its data structures. Opening Word documents? You *can* do that, with OpenOffice.org, but there's an application pending with the U.S. Patent and Trademark Office that may let Microsoft shut that down.

As for the electrical engineering simulations he'd originally bought the computer for? Those might be OK, but see page 63 for a list of patents that his simulations may inadvertently infringe if he calculates his Fourier transforms in certain manners. (His work frequently involves simulating integrated circuits, and he holds hardware patents 6,147,653 and 6,239,755. However, he has never written a video game.)

Another time, he mentioned that he was thinking about writing a package to do simulations for nonlinear optics problems, since there are none on the market now. "I'm safe using algorithms published in journal articles?" he asked. The answer is once again no. On page 88, I discuss a data compression method from a peer-reviewed journal that led to patent headaches for those who were foolish enough to apply a published mathematical algorithm without consulting a lawyer first. In my own statistical work, I make use of factor analysis reasonably often, but some methods of factor analysis are now covered by patent 6,807,536.

An entirely new economic arrangement has appeared in mathematics and its offspring, computer science. Before, we were free to do whatever our abilities allowed, since mathematical and computational results were in the public domain—nobody could own an idea. This arrangement worked to bring us the mathematical and computationally advanced world we live in today. But in the past decade, a new set of rules has been imposed: an individual can own a mathematical result that he or she has discovered and can sue those who do not ask permission to use that result—even if the other person independently derived it.

The ownership of mathematical algorithms is truly a new concept and engenders one of the main questions underlying economics and law: what can a single human being claim ownership of? Although people sometimes describe property ownership as "natural," it is clearly a social invention, designed to overcome economic and social problems. For example, the Earth was here 4.5 billion years before I was, and yet I am the sole owner of that piece of it that rests under my house. As a society, we have established this property right as a sensible solution to the sitcom-esque problems that would arise if anybody could show up at my home and use it as their own. Conversely, the benefits to private ownership of the sidewalk in front of my house are significantly fewer, so society has granted no one private ownership of it. There are other economic arguments for the ownership of abstractions like the design of a machine, which I discuss in this book.

The reader has no doubt been exposed to more than enough rhetoric about the fact that we live in an information age and our economic progress depends on the efficient movement and processing of information—and efficient information usage depends on better mathematical algorithms. But does inventing (and enforcing) the concept of ownership of a mathematical theorem make for a better economy? Is a mathematical algorithm more like a house or a sidewalk?

This is the first book to seriously ask whether it makes sense to allow for ownership of a computational algorithm. This question is not about the metaphysics of ownership, but about economic practicalities: because individuals can own the results of their research, they are more likely to innovate, but when you can't use the math without permission, implementing and using the innovations become more costly. Since the new protections are not unambiguously a plus, we have to do the cost-benefit analysis to determine whether the new innovation they bring about is worth the trouble they cause.

## The Credits

Thanks to the following people, who suffered through my illegible early drafts:

Robert Axtell, Derrick Higgins, and Guy Klemens (Computation)
Joseph Harrington and Brian Kahin (Economics)
Chris Kelaher, Mary Kwak, and Vicky Macintyre (Editorial issues)
Matthew Bye (Legal issues)
Derrick Higgins and Arika Okrent (Linguistics)
Josh Epstein, Carol Graham, and Peyton Young (Center on Social and Economic Dynamics)

# CHAPTER ONE

# Introduction

Now should software be protected from undue imitation and plagiarism? At present, all of the traditional means of protecting intellectual property (IP)—patents, copyright, and trade secrets—are applied to software in one manner or another, and the U.S. Congress has even invented a new type for cases in which these may be insufficient, via the Digital Millennium Copyright Act.

Software is not just like any other machine, as some courts have ruled, and it is not just *Hamlet* with numbers: it is a functional hybrid that can be duplicated at no cost, is legible by computers in some forms and by humans in others, and has a unique mathematical structure. All of these facts have to be taken into consideration in designing any type of IP protection for software.

## Patents

It has become a hobby among computer scientists to find the worst software patents granted. There are hundreds that make a competent programmer groan—and want to file for his or her own patents. For now, a single example will suffice to illustrate why software authors and users are so bothered by the state of patents today.

Patent 6,389,458, granted May 14, 2002 (filed October 30, 1998, by Brian Shuster), is for pop-up browser windows, which are typically used

1

**Figure 1-1. This Opens a New Window and Puts It in the Foreground**

```
function onExit(){
    popup = window.open("pop.html","Don't go!");
    popup.focus();}
```

by advertisers to put ads on top of the content that people actually want to see, and to make it difficult for users to leave a web site. Figure 1-1 shows the three lines of code required to implement the patent in JavaScript, a language included in web browsers since December 1995, although the patent also covers implementations in any other programming language, even ones that have not yet been invented.[1]

The U.S. Patent and Trademark Office (USPTO) deemed that this combination of one line of code to open a computer window and a subsequent line to focus on the window is a new, nonobvious invention, and that no persons may put these three lines of code in sequence in their own work unless they pay Shuster's company (Ideaflood, Inc.) a royalty for the privilege of doing so. In 2018 this combination of three lines will enter the public domain.[2]

### A Counterpoint

Here is the abstract for patent 4,314,081 (granted February 2, 1982, to Bryan Molloy and Klaus Schmiegel): "3-Aryloxy-3-phenylpropyl-amines and acid additions salts thereof, useful as psychotropic agents, particularly as anti-depressants." This patent covers the active ingredient in the formula for the antidepressant Prozac, shown in figure 1-2.

It is unlikely that even the best chemists could look at the chemical formula in figure 1-2 and infer that it could alleviate symptoms of depression in certain people. If they could, it would be because they had studied the work of Molloy and Schmiegel. Nor could we ask the best chemists to

1. For those who would like to infringe this patent on their own web pages: include the JavaScript from figure 1-1 and the tag `<BODY onUnload="onExit()">` in the HTML for the page.
2. A patent is valid for twenty years following the date when the application was filed. The patent can be viewed at the USPTO's website, www.uspto.gov. Given a patent number, the patent can also be downloaded from pat2pdf.org.

Figure 1-2. This Alleviates Depression

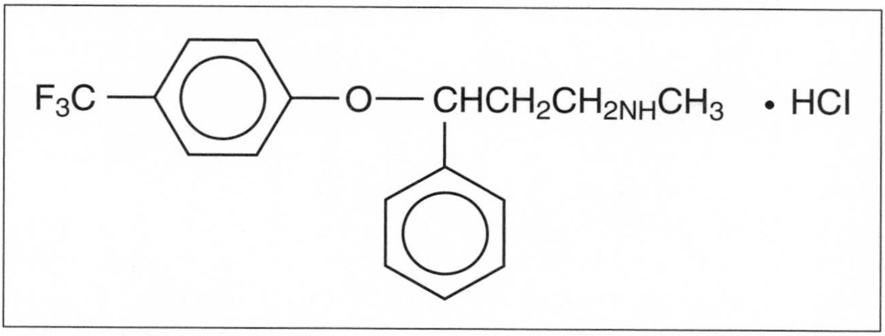

$F_3C$ —⟨benzene ring⟩— $O$ — $CHCH_2CH_2NHCH_3$ • $HCl$

Used with permission of Eli Lilly and Company.

quickly jot down a chemical compound to alleviate depression and expect them to produce anything like this formula, the product of years of research by Molloy and Schmiegel costing untold dollars. Conversely, Shuster's invention would make a good quiz question for an undergraduate computer science class. Nonetheless, the patent for Prozac and the patent for pop-ups are entirely equal under the law.

### A Persistent Problem

The pop-up patent is not an isolated case that slipped by an overworked patent examiner. Systematic differences in how software and machines or chemicals are constructed cause software patents to be systematically overbroad or obvious.

To paraphrase Socrates, the unexamined patent is not worth giving. Yet most software patent advocates claim as a platitudinous truth that software is just like any other technology. For example, in his 57-page review of IP protection for software, Kenneth Dam, Brookings scholar and IBM's former vice president of law and external relations, devotes one sentence to software versus physical patents: "In principle, the economic issues involved in software-related patents raise no economic issues other than those presented by patents generally."[3] He then discusses more general problems about the patenting system without a word of evidence to demonstrate that the economics of software is just like the economics of all other technologies.

3. Dam (1995).

If his claim were true, software patents would certainly make sense. In reality, the economics of software differs significantly from the economics of all other fields. Although some of software's problems have analogues in other industries (see chapter 5), many are almost entirely unique, notably the problems stemming from its mathematical properties, the structure of the software market, and the importance of interoperability (see chapters 3, 6, and 7, respectively).

Outside of a foolish consistency, there is no reason for patent law to ignore these unique features. If there were separate laws for physics- and chemistry-related inventions, the courts would be tied up for decades attempting to determine which laws applied where. But software is so clearly different from physical machines (I draw the line precisely and unambiguously in chapter 4) that the courts and USPTO could readily maintain an appropriately drawn line.

In assuming that there is no such difference and thus extending patent protection to software, courts have overlooked three important distinctions. First, a sufficiently detailed description of a computer program is the program itself, so it is sometimes difficult to distinguish between the idea and its implementation. For the pop-up window, the idea is a window that automatically opens and moves to the front when the user views a new page; the implementation is listed in figure 1-1. For Prozac, the idea is a selective serotonin reuptake inhibitor (SSRI); the implementation is shown in figure 1-2. Traditionally, patents have been granted to implementations of ideas and not to the ideas themselves—there are a dozen SSRIs on the market that did not infringe on the Prozac patent. But in software, the pattern has been reversed: most patents cover ideas like the pop-up window, regardless of implementation, so they tend to be too broad.

Second, a program is, in a literal sense, a piece of mathematics. This is not merely a play on words or a loose metaphor; a basic theorem of computer science demonstrates their equivalence. The courts agree that pure math is not patentable but that software is—yet the two are equivalent. The courts dumped the problem of reconciling the contradiction on the USPTO, which has resolved it by allowing patents on mathematical algorithms.

Third, vastly different categories of people write software. Nobody makes drugs but drug companies, so a patent on Prozac is a restriction only on other drug companies. But a patent on a piece of code is a restriction not only on software companies but also on the information technology department of every company in America, not to mention every person who writes macros to facilitate his or her work, or even students who (unlike chemistry students) could easily write a patent-infringing program and distribute it online.[4] Because software patents are a restriction not only on competitors but on a wide array of computer users, the cost-benefit analysis underlying patent law needs to be done anew for software.

### The Problem Has Come to the Fore

Although the argument thus far may seem abstract, the economic consequences of bad patents are very real. To date, the USPTO has granted between 170,000 and 200,000 software patents, and applications continue to flood in; each one of those issued gives the holder the right to sue others where no such right existed before.[5] Because independent invention is not a defense against claims of patent infringement, anyone working in front of a computer could be a target for a profitable infringement suit. Some entrepreneurs have responded to this bonanza of lucrative targets by creating businesses, such as Acacia Technologies, whose sole purpose is to buy software patents and sue companies for infringement.[6] Because the nature of the software writing process makes independent invention much more common than in other fields, opportunistic lawsuits have been more numerous as well.

In an interview with venture capitalists and software developers, Ronald Mann, co-director of the Center for Law, Business, and Economics at the University of Texas at Austin, repeatedly found a resigned attitude toward patents:

> Software patents are multiplying so rapidly that it is likely that many product startups that are developing ultimately will infringe patents held by large existing companies. . . . Several of my interview subjects

---

4. For example, when I graded papers for Caltech's undergraduate intellectual property class, students would often post their work online and send me a web link. Some of these exercises could be found by search engines such as Google and were therefore distributed to the world. In a computer science class, this method of handing in homework could easily be the worldwide distribution of a patent-infringing program.

5. The low estimate is by Greg Aharonian (editor of the Internet Patent News Service), personal communication, July 23, 2004; the high estimate is from Bessen and Hunt (2004a).

6. Cherry (2004).

joked that they thought it likely—without any investigation or particular knowledge—that there would be *something* in IBM's [patent] portfolio that their product infringed. . . .[7]

Potential innovators know that the large mass of existing patents held by IBM and Microsoft are likely to receive some share of revenues from any major new product.[8]

The burgeoning number of multimillion-dollar software patent disputes shows that this concern is not merely speculative. Some major disputes are between well-known firms such as Adobe and Macromedia, Yahoo! and Google, or Id Software and Creative Labs. Many others have pitted small firms in the business of lawsuits against large software companies, as in the suits of Acacia against nine cable companies; American Video Graphics against twelve video game vendors; British Technology Group against Amazon.com, Microsoft, Apple, and vendors of virus-detection software; Eolas against Microsoft; and DE Technologies against Dell.[9] The list goes on. Note well that none of these suits allege that the defendant read the plaintiff's work and then appropriated it without permission; in every case two groups independently arrived at the same algorithm, and the one with the patent sued the other.

Whether these claims are justified or not, each funnels millions of dollars out of research and design of better software and into the legal system. If nothing else, this book proposes clarifications of the rules on software patents so that disputes either do not arise or are settled efficiently.

## Free Software

Another noteworthy example is *Kodak* v. *Sun*. Sun developed the Java programming language (discussed further in chapter 7) and gives it away

7. Mann (2004, p. 53).
8. Mann (2004, p. 57).
9. On Acacia's suit, see p. 89; on AVG's suit, Fred Locklear, "Patent Aggregator Attempts to Make Tech and Game Giants Bleed," *Ars Technica*, November 5, 2004 (arstechnica.com/news.ars/post/20041105-4374.html); on *BTG* v. *Amazon*, Douglas Sorocco, "Amazon, Netflix, and Overstock Sued for Internet Visitor Tracking Patent Infringement," *PHOSITA*, September 17, 2004 (www.okpatents.com/phosita/archives/2004/09/amazon_netflix.html); on *BTG* v. *Apple* and *MSFT*, John Oates, "BTG Sues Apple and MS over Software Downloads," *The Register*, July 21, 2004 (www.theregister.co.uk/2004/07/21/btg_sues_apple_microsoft/); on BTG and virus detection, "UK Firm Patents Software Downloads," *The Register*, June 16, 2004 (www.theregister.co.uk/2004/06/16/uk_

for free, in the hopes that it will expand the company's hardware sales. Kodak proved to a court that Sun was infringing on a handful of patents that Kodak had bought from Wang Laboratories (now Unisys) and then settled with Sun for $92 million dollars in damages—from *free* software.[10]

Although free and open software has become an increasing part of the business strategies of many companies and even of governments from Munich to Delaware to Venezuela, Kodak has proved that any such decision brings a liability risk.[11] One group found that the Linux kernel, the most high profile piece of open software and one of the most widely used, potentially infringes 283 patents.[12] Under such circumstances, businesses and governments may be reluctant to take advantage of the public good that Linux's developers have created—the city of Munich has already put a brief delay in its Linux migration plans because of concerns about fifty patents on inventions such as browsers that allow navigation with the <tab> key (see figure 2-4).[13] In the United States, the Department of Defense, Census Bureau, and National Aeronautics and Space Administration are all involved in open-source projects, saving taxpayers money over proprietary alternatives—but what happens if a patent-holder sues the Department of Defense for infringement?[14] The potential liability from free software written in-house or by others could cost taxpayers even more than the $92 million Sun paid out.

firm_patents_downloads/); on *Eolas* v. *MSFT,* p. 86; and on *DE Technologies* v. *Dell,* Tony Smith, "Dell Sued for Alleged Global Sales Patent Abuse," *The Register,* November 5, 2004 (www.theregister.co.uk/2004/11/05/dell_e-commerce_patent_clash/).

10. Ashlee Vance, "Sun Settles Java Spat with Kodak for $92 Million," *The Register,* October 7, 2004 (www.theregister.co.uk/2004/10/07/kodak_sun_settle/). See also the pre-settlement report, John Oates, "Kodak Wins Sun Java Patents Case, Wants $1bn," *The Register,* October 4, 2004 (www.theregister.co.uk/2004/10/04/kodak_wins_java/).

11. Other countries that mandate the use of open-source software in government include Argentina, Brazil, Bulgaria, Chile, Colombia, France, Italy, and Peru. Countries that have a stated "preference" for open source include Bahrain, Belgium, China and Hong Kong, Costa Rica, France, Germany, Iceland, Israel, Italy, Malaysia, Poland, Portugal, Philippines, and South Africa. Robin Bloor, "The Government Open Source Dynamic," *The Register,* January 7, 2005 (www.theregister.co.uk/2005/01/07/gov_open_source_dynamic/). On Delaware and Munich, see Galli (2003).

12. Stephen Shankland, "Group: Linux Potentially Infringes 283 Patents," *CNET News.com,* August 1, 2004 (news.zdnet.com/2100-3513_22-5291403.html). Notice that the study is by a firm that sells IP lawsuit insurance, so the number is likely to be biased upward. Nonetheless, the exact number is not important: the entire project could conceivably be shut down by one or two key patents.

13. Patentrecherche Linux-Basisclient München (www.presseportal.de/showbin.htx?id=31139&type=document [German pdf]).

14. Galli (2003).

## Copyright

The correct breadth of a patent, in the legal and economic sense, covers the details of an idea's implementation, not the broad idea itself. For software, that means lines of text. Copyright, which also protects text, has a few major advantages over patents, notably regarding independent authorship.

If users cut and paste another person's code into their own without permission, that act is a clear-cut copyright violation. But what if two people independently write the same code? A thousand monkeys with typewriters would need a thousand years to hammer out an exact copy of *Hamlet*, but if two programmers needing a pop-up window both wrote code exactly matching that in figure 1-1, it would be no surprise at all. In the patent world, every such coincidence is a lawsuit in the making; in a copyright regime, multiple inventors will not be able to harass each other, because independent authorship is indeed a valid defense for copyright cases.

On the other hand, whereas two bodies of code that look alike may have been independently invented, a body of code that looks nothing like another may be a direct plagiarism with a trivial translation. There needs to be a mechanism in place to facilitate verification of independent invention, which can be done via inspection of the process by which a given program has been written. The details of how copyright should be applied to code are discussed in chapter 8.

## Politics

The primary policy recommendation of this book is that the U.S. Congress needs to consider what sort of IP protection is appropriate for software. To date, the law governing software has been entirely written by the courts, which do not have the authority to settle policy questions, only to interpret the intent of Congress, as made clear in the dissenting opinion in *Diamond* v. *Diehr* (discussed in chapter 4): "The broad question whether computer programs should be given patent protection involves policy considerations that this Court [the Supreme Court] is not authorized to address." The Congress therefore needs to decide the optimal policy for software. I hope that this book will provide a good start for the debate.

The European Union recently concluded a heated battle over the patentability of "computer-implemented inventions" in its legislature. After years of fierce debates and protests, no law of any sort was passed; the parties are now preparing for the next round. Unfortunately, I cannot include discussion about the battle, because political events move so quickly that whatever I write will not be current by the time this book reaches print. Instead, I have focused on the more universal topics of patent policy from a mathematical and economic perspective. The case law in chapter 4 is U.S.-specific, but the European Patent Office accepts the same "general-purpose computer with software" wording trick that I discuss extensively and faces the same fundamental questions about the patentability of mathematics and software. Thus although I will not explicitly discuss the European debate, this book has immediate relevance to it.

Another battleground is in trade-related intellectual property (TRIP), and here too I avoid the ensuing international relations issues, which pertain largely to the harmonization of laws in different countries. As a practical matter, this means persuading others that they need to adopt U.S. IP law as their own, so if the United States adopts a patent policy that is ill conceived, trade negotiations may spread this policy the world over. Again, the politics of TRIP negotiation is ever changing, but the economics of good patent policy as discussed in this book is not.

## About the Book

A proper discussion of software IP will gather together perspectives from law, computer science, mathematics, and economics. This book is intended to provide a discussion of software intellectual property in all of its relevant contexts.

The first considered here is the economic perspective. Chapter 2 opens with an overview of patents and copyrights and then turns to the most important economic question about their design: how broad should protection be? That is, should an innovator have protection only from direct plagiarism, or from more loose imitation?

Focusing on the computer science side, chapter 3 examines the structure of software—the layers upon layers of complexity that have evolved to make it easier and easier for programmers to write useful programs. This chapter also introduces the mathematical context, explaining the extent to which mathematics and computer science overlap.

Chapter 4 explores the legal context through a history of how the courts have dealt with software. As in the mathematical context, software falls somewhere along a continuous spectrum of invention between physical machines, which should be patentable, and pure math, which should not be. Exactly where should the legal line between the patentable and the unpatentable be drawn? Since judges are knowledgeable about law but light on computer science, it is no surprise that the line drawn by the courts has proved to be in entirely the wrong place.

Chapter 5 elaborates on this question in the business context. Now that we have a firm rule about what may be patented, what are its effects on business and innovation in the real world? Is there evidence that it has led to more innovation than it has stifled? (Hint: no.)

Among the producers of patented goods, the software industry is unique in an interesting way: it is rather evenly split between those who make money by writing software for hire (that is, a labor market) and those who make money selling software via shrink-wrapped CDs (that is, a goods market). Patents do not affect both sides of the market equally. Chapter 6 discusses the bifurcated market and how patents shift the balance between the two sides.

The music and movie industries offer another important perspective on software, covered in chapter 7. The debate over what constitutes fair use of media is not one that I touch upon here, but that debate has spilled over into important issues of software protection. If a music label invents a special encoding for its music and distributes a program with which to play it, do users have the right to write their own software that can decode the music without the permission of the label? The current answer, according to the U.S. Congress, is that users do not have such a right. But since encryption and copy protection are so hard to define and delimit, this rule has turned into the broadest possible form of IP protection: once a software author has claimed that his or her work implements a copy protection scheme, that author can claim exclusive ownership of the right to produce any of a variety of add-ons, extensions, and accessories. No software is an island, entire of itself, so the ability to block competitors from producing interoperable software is an immense power that can be readily abused. Such abuses have already appeared in the courts, creating still more IP headaches for anyone who writes software, be it for music, electronic books, or garage-door openers.

Chapter 8 considers software as a literary work—*Hamlet* with numbers. As already mentioned, the process of writing a play and the process of writing a program are obviously very different, and IP rules need to take that into account. For those who have read this far and still believe that patents are appropriate, I offer suggestions on how patents can accommodate inventions-in-words. The natural protection for words on paper is copyright, but this too is not quite a perfect fit, so I also discuss how copyright for software could be more effectively implemented.

Chapter 9 collects and summarizes the policy recommendations from all of these perspectives.

# CHAPTER TWO

# Optimal Breadth

The foremost economic question surrounding patents and copyright is how much territory they should cover. Part of the answer lies in the function that patents serve, which is to enable the inventor to recoup profits from up-front investment in research. One person or company may invest the money to develop and test a new method or machine, but once research results are made public, competitors can use them with a significantly smaller investment. With multiple competitors providing identical products, the unit price for the product will fall until it is near the cost of producing that unit—meaning the immediate cost that competitors must spend, excluding the research costs the original inventor had invested.

If a company expects such a story to unfold from investing in and producing a new invention, it will never make the initial investment in research. By giving inventors a limited right to exclude others from copying their innovations, a patent makes it possible for them to keep prices on their invention high enough to hopefully recoup their investment costs.

## The Basics

Generally, a patent may be awarded for any novel, useful, and nonobvious machine, process, or composition of matter. It grants the holder the right to exclude other people from manufacturing the patented object or using the patented process for twenty years after the patent has been applied for.[1] If another party should do so, the patent-holder may sue. The suit will begin in the U.S. district courts, which hear a broad range of cases involving federal law. Appeals past the district courts would be heard by the Court of Appeals for the Federal Circuit, which hears a narrower range of cases. Further appeals go to the U.S. Supreme Court, but it is generally not interested in cases on subjects as bureaucratic as patent law. Another option for the defendant is to have the U.S. Patent and Trademark Office (USPTO) re-review the patent, but many restrictions apply to such reviews, and few patents are completely overturned. If the review is granted, some of the claims may be eliminated or narrowed.

### What a Patent Covers

The main part of a patent consists of a detailed list of claims, each for a very specific feature or piece of the mechanism. One patent usually includes dozens or even hundreds of claims, which add up to describe the entire invention. Typically, applicants' claims are as broad as possible, covering as many means of carrying out a step and as many of its applications as possible. After a search of prior works, examiners may propose that the claim be made narrower (or eliminated entirely) if they find it is not inventive as described. Through such negotiations, a patent is finally assembled. The item-by-item review is time-consuming, especially since examiners work on an innocent-until-proven-guilty basis: they may not reject a claim unless they have positive proof that it has already been made by another party.[2]

Some people believe that a patent covers a new idea, but this is not the case: it covers only the physical machine, composition, or process implementing that new idea, as described by the detailed claims. In practice the patent covers a mix of idea and implementation, since the two are never truly separable.

Independent invention is not a defense against claims of patent infringement. If a new inventor's idea and designs are along the same lines as those of a prior patent-holder, then the new inventor is still infringing on the patent, even if the two inventors have never communicated. Once

1. 35 U.S.C. §154 (a)(2).
2. Formally, there are more requirements: the enablement requirement, the utility requirement, the nonobviousness requirement. However, over the course of the book the reader will see that these other requirements have been weakened to the point of irrelevance.

the patent is in the public record, all inventors in the relevant field are presumed to be familiar with the work.

Since the designs do not have to be identical and the idea itself is not patented, their details must be compared to determine whether a new implementation is an infringement of the prior one. Inventors therefore have some leeway to "invent around" a prior invention and implement the same idea in a new way. This is not a problem for the issue of fostering innovation at the head of this chapter: if two producers are producing goods that are not identical, then unit prices will not necessarily be driven to unit costs, and all may be able to make a reasonable profit. For example, one design may be better suited to industrial applications and the other to consumer use.

### The Basics of Copyright

The intent of copyright is the same as for patents: authors must invest a great deal up front and hence need some sort of protection if they are to recoup that investment. Copyright is paperwork-free: a few words written on the proverbial cocktail napkin are automatically copyrighted. Copyright is far easier to obtain than a patent because it is much less powerful in a key respect: independent authorship is a valid defense against claims of copyright infringement. If two authors happen to write in a style so similar that one author's work seems to be a copy of the other, there is no violation of copyright—unless it can be proved that the second author had seen the first author's work and directly imitated it.

A copyright covers only the expression of an idea, never the idea itself. However, the expression of an idea is open to broad interpretation beyond strict plagiarism. It includes *derivative works*, which may be broadly or narrowly defined. For example, a recognizable character such as Darth Vader or Jerry Seinfeld may have copyright protection, even if the imitator is depicted in a different context and never directly quotes the original.

Topps, a chewing gum and trading card company, put out a line of cards named the Garbage Pail Kids that made fun of the Cabbage Patch Kids line of dolls. The names seemed similar, and the Garbage Pail Kids had the same dimpled cheeks and cabbage-sized heads as the dolls. The courts ruled that this passing resemblance and vaguely similar name were enough to constitute copyright infringement.[3]

3. *Original Appalachian Artworks, Inc.* v. *Topps Chewing Gum, Inc.*, 642 F. Supp. 1031 (N.D. Ga. 1986).

**Figure 2-1. Copyright Infringement Does Not Have to Be Literal**

A similar case involved Saul Steinberg's 1976 cover cartoon for the *New Yorker* depicting the New Yorker's view of the world (see figure 2-1). It showed four Manhattan blocks in great detail, the rest of the United States as a flat plane interrupted by a few cities and protruding rocks, the Pacific Ocean as a narrow band, and the rest of the world as a mere strip on the horizon. The one-sheet poster for the film *Moscow on the Hudson* consisted of line drawings of the movie's three main characters beneath a detailed view of four Manhattan blocks, then a strip labeled "Atlantic Ocean," and in the distance a flat plane with a few European cities in caricature. This is clearly not a literal copy—at the least, one faces West and the other East—but the court ruled that it nonetheless infringed Steinberg's copyright.[4]

Thus although the U.S. Code stipulates that copyright includes only the expression of an idea and not the idea itself, the courts do not follow a strictly literal interpretation when deciding where to draw the line. By allowing a broader protection, they leave open the same question as for patents: what is the economically optimal breadth of protection?

4. *Steinberg* v. *Columbia Pictures Industries, Inc.*, 663 F. Supp. 706 (S.D.N.Y. 1987).

## Maximizing the Size of the Market

For both patents and copyrights, the key economic question is whether they should cover only one implementation (as in the case of Prozac) or a broader class (such as selective serotonin reuptake inhibitors). How different must a cartoon be before it is not infringing the copyright of another?

### Patent Length

This discussion concentrates on the optimal breadth of protection for intellectual property (IP), not the optimal number of years for which protection should be valid. By contrast, the academic literature concerns itself more with length of protection, if only because length can be easily defined and measured, whereas there is no metric for breadth.[5]

Since the software market operates at famously rapid speed, the length of a patent is effectively infinite. Some propose that patents on software should expire more quickly than the standard 20 years, perhaps after 2 or 3 years. But even if a patent were to last for a single day after being granted, the issue would remain because many patent protections are retroactive to when the patent was first filed. Since a savvy applicant can keep a patent lingering on USPTO desks for the better part of a decade (the so-called *submarine patent*; see chapter 5), the only way to achieve truly short durations would be to allow some patents to expire before they are granted. This poses a few practical difficulties, to say the least.

Some argue that software should be covered by copyright instead of patents, but copyright protection lasts decades longer than for patents. As demonstrated by the many authors who write poetry in the Perl programming language, there is no clear line between expression in code and artistic expression, so there is no way to write a robust copyright law that gives code brief protection and prose long protection. Hence I assume that protection on code is effectively infinite and focus on the breadth of IP protection.[6]

5. Many theoretical papers also discuss the trade-off between patent length and breadth, such as Klemperer (1990) and those papers discussed therein.

6. The academic literature, such as Klemperer (1990), is generally in agreement that a patent of (effectively) infinite duration should be infinitely narrow, proving this via dynamic optimization for infinitely lived agents. By contrast, my argument in this chapter is based on maximizing the size of the market. The key assumption linking my argument with the existing literature is that deadweight loss is a decreasing function of the number of providers.

### Balancing Breadth

One may think of the economic goal of a patent as maximizing the number of people providing a good. (Although I use patent-oriented terminology here, the same analysis holds for copyrights.) This formulation subsumes the typical "patents foster innovation" story: if zero people provided an item without a patent, then allowing the item to be patented would raise the number of providers to one and would be a good thing. But beyond this, if many people provided the item without patents, then the patent would be an impediment, lowering the number of providers from many to one.

Suppose that a company has just invented a new product, expending $R$ dollars in one-time research costs to develop it, and suppose that the cost of implementing a production line is $I_o$. Also assume that once the new product is put out, all the ideas it embodies will be common knowledge. Now let $I_{np}$ be the cost that a competitor would have to expend to implement a competing product, having seen how the innovative company did it, and given that there is no patent on the invention. Let $I_p$ be the cost a competitor would have to expend to implement its product given that the original innovation is patented. The patent makes copying difficult (that is, it engenders *incomplete appropriability*), raising the cost of production, so $I_p > I_{np}$.[7] Economists will be disappointed that the model is so sparsely specified, but other readers will be relieved that the notation contains only these four variables.

First, notice that $I_p$ is usually not infinite: since a patent is for the implementation of an idea and not the idea itself, others may invent alternative implementations and offer competing products that are comparable to but different from the original. If a patent is sufficiently broad, however, any sort of competing product would be infringing. So to maximize the number of producers, $I_p$ should be large, but not *too* large.

It is often the case that $R + I_o > I_p > I_{np}$, meaning that the first company must exert more time and effort than the competitors, patent or not. This is the natural course of a market's development: people learn from each other, and every day things get easier. In fact, even without $R$ it is sometimes the case that $I_o > I_p$. Every market has a first entrant, even though the first entrant is likely to be trampled by imitators who can make a cheaper and possibly better product. For example, the first portable MP3

---

7. Landes and Posner (2003, p. 299).

**Figure 2-2. A Good Patent Follows Two Simple Guidelines**

---

*The notation*:

$R$:    Research costs

$I_o$:    The inventor's production costs

$I_{np}$:    The imitator's production costs with no patents

$I_p$:    The imitator's production costs with patents

*The guidelines*:

1. Patents are necessary only when $I_{np}$ is significantly smaller than $R + I_o$.

2. If $I_p$ approaches infinity, then the patent is too broad.

---

player was made by Saehan/Eiger Labs, which was trampled by Diamond's Rio, which was in turn trampled by Apple's iPod. Yet all of these companies fared well.[8] Patents make sense only when $R + I_o$ is *significantly* larger than $I_{np}$, meaning that the initial entrant expects to be trampled by imitators to such an extent that it will never recoup the expenditure of $R$. So $I_{np}$ may be smaller than $R + I_o$, but if it is *too much* smaller, then no one will invest $R$ without patent protection. Figure 2-2 summarizes the two market-maximizing criteria discussed to this point. They are already sufficient to evaluate a wide range of patents.

### A Good Patent May Raise Competitors' Costs

Historically, as mentioned earlier, patents have been for a machine or process that implements an idea, not the idea itself. Prozac interfaces with serotonin receptors in the human brain. Eli Lilly did not have a patent on that interface, so a dozen other brands have the same interface, implemented with a different drug. Others have implemented competing products that did not violate Prozac's patent, demonstrating that $I_p$ is low enough that criterion 2 is not violated.

---

8. Diamond and Apple are better known than Eiger Labs, whose legacy persists in products such as Compaq's iPaq MP3 player.

If there were no patent on Prozac's active molecule, then imitators' implementation costs would be vanishingly small in relation to the years of work represented by $R$. As a first approximation, one may as well set $I_{np} \approx 0$, since Eli Lilly wrote the whole blueprint and now the imitators have only to execute it. When $I_{np} \approx 0$, it is obviously the case that $R + I_o \gg I_{np}$, so Eli Lilly would never spend $R$. By criterion 1, there is a valid need for a patent.

The Prozac patent is thus in harmony with both criteria and thus fosters competition rather than stifles it. After the patent, competitors must now spend large quantities on $I_p$; it is probably still the case that $R + I_o > I_p$, but the gap is hopefully small enough so that the first entrant will survive on the market and be willing ex ante to invest $R$. This is the ideal of how the patenting scheme would work.

### But a Good Patent Does Not Raise Competitors' Costs to Infinity

Now consider the counterfactual case in which the idea of an SSRI is the exclusive property of Eli Lilly. Then no other competitor may enter the market—in effect, the cost of implementation for a competitor has risen to $I_p = \infty$. Clearly, this is overkill.

In my refrigerator, all the containers have patent numbers. Newspring's sealed container (patents 6,056,138 and 6,196,404) is evidently different from Rubbermaid's (patents pending), which is different again from Tupperware's (including patents 5,974,686 and 6,035,769). If Tupperware held a patent on the concept of an airtight container, I would not have such a clutter in the fridge. Instead, the best it could do was patent its own implementation of an airtight container, on the basis of its specific materials and design. Because the USPTO selected the appropriate breadth of patents, a dozen distinct implementations flourish.

Or imagine a world in which only one company could make portable music players, and there is only one brand of cellular phone. If Sony or Qualcomm had sufficiently broad patents, this would be the case; fortunately, their actual patents are for specific implementations of broad ideas, so competitors can still enter with distinct products.

The goal of the patent-seeker is to obtain as broad a patent as possible. However, such a broad monopoly violates criterion 2 and is bad for society. The social optimum is a patent that is just broad enough to ensure that $I_p \approx R + I_o$, meaning that the patent-seeker is able to successfully compete and thus has sufficient incentive to invest $R$.

## Figure 2-3. The Banana Protective Device: The Fugitive Fermentation of an Individual Brain

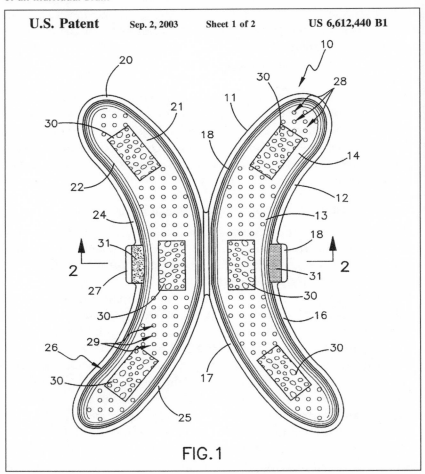

FIG. 1

*Low Research Cost Patents (R = 0)*

Many patents (if not most) are what Thomas Jefferson would perhaps call "the fugitive fermentation of an individual brain," an example being the Banana Protective Device, patent 6,612,440 (to David Agulnik, September 2, 2003), pictured in figure 2-3.[9] I am personally dubious that it

9. See p. 46 for the entire quotation.

took years of research to devise the invention—$R$ approaches zero here. If free riders take the idea of a banana case and produce their own, Agulnik is deprived of the profits not from millions of dollars in research but from a few minutes' thought.

As much as the flash of an idea may deserve or merit protection, there is no *economic* reason to afford it any protection at all. Since $R$ is zero, one may rewrite $R + I_o$ as just $I_o$, and there is every reason to expect that $I_o = I_{np}$. That is, it will cost competitors about as much as it cost Agulnik to produce a banana case. By market-maximizing criterion 1, there is little or no justification for a patent: Agulnik and all others can compete in the marketplace without government intervention.

Another way to approach the patent would be to redefine the invention: Agulnik did not invent the idea of a banana protective device but the very specific device pictured in figure 2-3. He may have made hundreds of attempts to get the size of the air holes just right, to select the optimal curvature of the case, and so on, and those hundreds of experiments may deserve protection. By this reading, the patent meets the criteria for a good patent, but it should only be broad enough to protect those details of implementation that cost Agulnik time and effort.[10]

### An Example in Software

Figure 2-4 shows the essence of patent 6,785,865, assigned to Microsoft Corporation, for "Discoverability and navigation of hyperlinks via tabs." As the patent explains, it is often difficult to determine what elements on a web page are links, since some links are hidden under pictures or otherwise obscured; the patent solves this problem by allowing the user to hit the <tab> key to go from one link to another.

Figure 2-4 shows the core of the patent: the detailed textual description provides minimal additional detail. Notably, there is no computer code to explain how the list of links is maintained, how focus is allocated, and so on.[11]

The idea is that a browser lets the user move through the document using the <tab> key. Given this idea, anyone could construct the flowchart

10. There are, in fact, competing banana protective devices on the market. The one described here is sold as the Banana Guard. Meanwhile, the halves of the Banana Bunker open by sliding along the length of the banana, and therefore the implementation differs considerably from this patent. See bananaguard.com or bananabunker.com for details.

11. There is some additional detail about how the shape of the link's outline is determined when the link is a picture; again, it is not in the form of code, but another flowchart.

**Figure 2-4. Tab Browsing Flowchart**

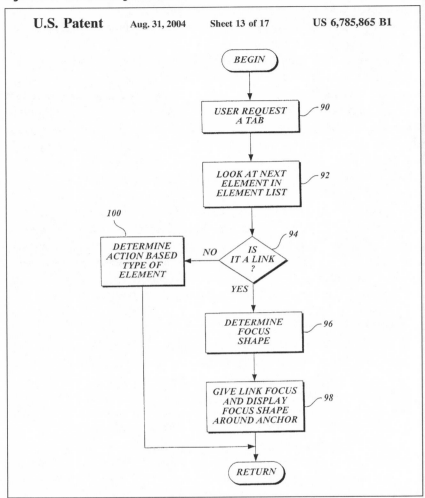

at the level of detail of figure 2-4. This exercise does not compare with the amount of labor coding, testing, debugging, and recoding that went into the invention. The details of implementation analogous to the holes and curvature of the banana protective device or the chemical formula for Prozac are nowhere to be found.

If the patent is for the idea instead of the line-by-line implementation, as in this case, any implementation of the flowchart will infringe the patent—and it would be difficult to design a browser that did not some-how do so. Opera, Safari, Mozilla, Firefox, Lynx, Links, Camino, and any other non-Microsoft browser are likely infringing the patent.[12] Because the wording of the patent is so vague, it fails to meet both crite-rion 1 (since $R$ for what is written in the patent is zero) and criterion 2 (since it needlessly blocks competitors from producing anything that fol-lows this very broad flowchart). An appropriate heuristic for the case of software is that the toil goes into the implementation of the idea, and hence that the implementation deserves protection, not the broad idea.

12. As well as being a prime example of a patent that is too broad, it also shows how the search for prior art can fail: Microsoft cited 24 patents and 1 article as prior art, and the examiner added 4 more articles, but no mention is made of any other software. For exam-ple, the Lynx browser allowed <tab>-based browsing through text for five years before the patent was granted and may have served as prior art for many of the patent's claims. See chapter 5 for more on the problem of software prior art.

# CHAPTER THREE

# From Equations to Software

There is no magic or genius to the process of programming, just small components built upon larger structures, and then still larger structures built upon those. Isaac Newton explained that he progressed by standing on the shoulders of giants, but perhaps a more appropriate metaphor for software development is that modern computing rests on the back of a giant turtle, which rests on the back of another turtle, which rests on another turtle. . . . [1]

## A Summary for Non-Geeks

I have come to realize, over the course of many parties and dates, that some people do not like hearing about the details of computer programming. For them, I offer this summary of the important points that are relevant to the law and the economics of software patents.

---

1. No mythology claims that the earth rests on an infinite pile of turtles. A few Native American stories surmise that North America rests on the back of a giant turtle; and a Hindi myth explains that the earth rests on an elephant, which rests on a turtle. Dr. Seuss's *Yertle the Turtle* is about a tyrannical turtle king who commands his turtles to form a tower so that he can survey his kingdom; and there is a joke, often attributed to Stephen Hawking, about a flat-earther who insists that the earth rests on a turtle, and when asked what the turtle is standing on, she exclaims, "It's turtles all the way down!"

### State Machines versus Purpose-Built Circuits

When the digital processors in dollar-store calculators, digital clocks, and microwave ovens leave the factory, they are set up to do only a few things, which are enabled by burning circuits into the machine's circuit board. By contrast, the processors of modern computers are designed to do a great variety of things if put into different states—that is, repro-grammed—by the user. In computer science terminology, they are *state machines*. It is possible to change their state because computers are built to respond in given ways to sequences of coded instructions known as programs. There is little if any gray area between the program changing the state of a computer and the computer itself (the state machine). The state machine is a device that is burnt into place at the factory; its states can be reconfigured at will by the user.

### A Program Consists of Nothing but Data Structures and Functions

Computer programs are constructed using formal systems of symbols known as programming languages. The coded instructions that make up a program break down into data structures and functions. The data struc-tures are simply a formal means of organizing data. Functions are the verbs of programming languages, and they translate directly into algo-rithms. A good data structure allows a program to efficiently process information internally and make coherent external records of data for future use. For example, word processor documents are complex data structures that encode all the information needed to assemble those doc-uments and transmit them in the form of a stream of ones and zeros to a hard drive. If another program can understand the data structure, then it can edit or display the document encoded into the file and interoperate with the original word processor.

### Any Program Can Be Translated into Virtually Any Programming Language

Translating from one language to another is *trivial*, and unlike trans-lating from French to English, say, it can be done exactly.[2] That is, pro-gramming languages are not equivalent in the colloquial sense of being very similar but in the formal mathematical sense, just as $(3 \times 2)$ and 6 are equivalent.

---

2. Italicized technical terms are defined in the glossary at the back of this book.

### A Program Such as a Word Processor or Spreadsheet Defines a Language

Under the hood, the typical word processor or spreadsheet is nothing but a multitude of functions, each doing a specialized task like calculating the placement of words on a page or of widgets on the screen. Those functions also define a specialized language. Although this book does not cover the graphic design issues connected with user-oriented software, those parts of such a program that fall under patent law can be trivially translated into any traditional programming language.

### There Is No Distinction between Code and Mathematics

Beyond the fact that most programming languages readily translate into other such languages, they can also be translated into a method of writing pure mathematical functions known as the *lambda calculus*. Running a program and evaluating its functional equivalent are identical processes, as demonstrated in 1936 in a set of mathematical results now known as the Church-Turing thesis.

The three points just outlined indicate a massive equivalence: any functionality of a computer, be it an exotic new programming language or a word processor, is equivalent to a mathematical expression. Where is the line between software and mathematics? Mathematicians Alonzo Church and Alan Turing proved that there is none—in 1936, no less.

### Independent Invention Is Common on an Algorithmic Level, but the Details of Implementation Rarely Match

There are hundreds of proofs of the Pythagorean theorem, but most of them fall into a few categories—given the problem statement and the tools available to prove it, even the most creative human brain will follow certain paths in going from the problem statement to a solution. However, just as there are hundreds of ways to express an idea in English or any other language, there are hundreds of ways to implement an algorithm using any of the hundreds of programming languages in which it can be expressed. Generally, if a designer can write a sufficiently detailed explanation of what a program should do, then it is a trivial process to implement it in computer code—but writing a *good* implementation is far from trivial.

### Programmers Try to Keep the Interface and Its Implementation Separate

The central principle that makes it possible to write software code easily is that each component at each level of a program's structure has an interface and an implementation. The interface is what the component's user would see: it could be the inputs and outputs to a function, or it could be what appears on the screen of an application. The implementation is the hidden inner workings: for a function, this consists of the steps that turn the input into output, and for an application, it is the functions that the program calls on at the user's request. Here is a simple rule of thumb: protecting the interface will prove to be economically detrimental; therefore any protection for software should apply to an author's implementation. The remainder of this chapter will give a more detailed overview of the interface-implementation pairs on each level of the structure, and the legal and economic implications of their design.

## The Lowest Level

At its lowest level, the software edifice rests on an electronic foundation: the *transistor*, a device that is used to control the flow of electricity in electronic equipment and that consists of a semiconductor with three electrodes. Two of these are inputs and one an output. If (and only if) both inputs receive an electrical charge, then the output will emit a charge. Historically, there have been other implementations of the same idea—notably vacuum tubes, which have the same two-in, one-out property but require much more power and produce much more heat in the process. Many considerations of materials science and electronics go into the production of a good transistor: its inputs have different voltages, its materials must be the best semiconductors, and the heat it produces can destroy the transistor if not vented properly—especially if the designer has found a way to cram a million of them into a square centimeter.

To the logician, the transistor is the electronic equivalent of an AND gate: both input one *and* input two must be on (or "true") in order to have output (which is then also true), but if either input is false, the output is false. It is also possible to construct an element in which the output is on if either input one *or* input two is on, an arrangement that is naturally called the OR gate. To illustrate, twist two wires together to form a Y, the top of the Y being the two inputs. If a current passes along one or the other, then current will flow out of the bottom of the Y. With enough wire and transistors and a bit of ingenuity, the electrical equivalent of any logical expression can be constructed by tying together enough transistors.[3]

3. The astute reader will note that it is impossible to tie together ANDs and ORs to form a NOT, but a pair of wires and a transistor is still all one needs to make a NOT gate. First,

Binary notation allows all numbers to be represented by a series of ones and zeros; for example, three becomes 011 and four becomes 100. Adding two numbers becomes a series of logic problems: in the decimal system, 3 + 4 = 7; in the binary system, 011 + 100 = 111; and in logic (false, true, true) + (true, false, false) = (true, true, true). Since binary notation turns arithmetic into a logic problem, and the appropriate tangle of transistors can turn a logic problem into an electrical circuit, one could design a circuit to execute familiar arithmetic calculations.

A few standard circuit elements, sometimes referred to as *registers*, appear in every basic textbook on digital circuit design. Among the more common ones are the INCREMENT register, which will take in a set of signals representing a number and put out a set of signals representing that number plus one, and the ADD register, which will take in two streams of input and put out a stream representing their sum. Think of these registers as black boxes with a few input wires and a few output wires. The box could contain a tangle of transistors and resistors that implement the logic, or it could contain vacuum tubes, but there is no need to be concerned with such details. All an engineer needs to know in order to use the black box is what will come out along the output wires when any given signal is sent down the input wires.

Another standard circuit is the MEMORY register, a feedback loop of a few transistors. If the loop is set to a true state, it will stay in that state as long as electrical current is flowing through it. But if it is sent a signal to switch to a false state, then the feedback loop will switch accordingly and stay in the false state until another signal is sent to switch back to a true state.

Electronic components such as video screens and speakers follow a similar model. They are designed to produce an image, sound, or motion

---

define one input to the transistor to be the input to the NOT gate. Instead of reading the output of the transistor, just send it to ground. Now twist together two wires: define one arm of the Y to be the output for the NOT gate, and tie the other arm to the transistor's second input. Finally, run a constant current into the base of the Y. Now, if the input to the gate (going into the transistor) is true, then the constant current from the base of the Y will flow through the transistor to ground, so there will be no current along the gate's output; the gate thus outputs false when the input is true. If the gate's input is false, then no current flows through the transistor, so all current takes the other route down the Y, to the gate's output; the gate thus outputs true when the input is false. Thus, this configuration works as a NOT gate. Given ANDs, ORs, and NOTs, one can readily construct any logical expression, all of which can be made using enough transistors and wires.

when their registers are set to appropriate values.[4] Thus video and audio transmission readily translates into exercises in math and logic as well, which in essence consist of combining simple logic gates to form complex logic circuits.

These structures can be used to build a computing machine such as the average dollar-store calculator, which is simply a box of registers. When the user enters a number, it is placed into a MEMORY register. Then when the user presses the "square" button, that number is replicated to another MEMORY register, and the two are sent to a MULTIPLY register. Finally, a series of similar registers translates the result into signals to the calculator's screen so that the human user can read the output.

This is how the machines of old functioned, before general-purpose processors became so cheap. An engineer would design a circuit for the task at hand and then begin soldering together the appropriate physical components to implement the logic. This is still the cheapest way to construct single-use computers such as microwave ovens or digital watches, and it is still the best way to produce optimized devices for situations in which every nanosecond counts. It is in effect a one-step process that inextricably binds the design of the logic to the design of the machine itself, which will prove to have implications for the legal discussion in chapter 4.

## Turing's Machine

The innovation that facilitated the development of the next level of the edifice was simultaneously described in 1936 by Alonzo Church and Alan Turing.[5] Church's more abstract version is taken up later in the chapter. Turing's idea was based on a theoretical calculating machine. The Turing machine comprises a line of cells of indefinite length known as a tape; an active element called a head, which can move from cell to cell and can

4. A nice example would be Motorola or TI chip SN74LS248, which takes a binary-coded decimal input and drives a seven-segment display of the type found on dollar-store calculators. The data sheet, commonly available online, explicitly lists the logic necessary to convert electrical signals into human-readable numbers.

5. For a readable account of their work, see Davis (2000). The original sources, regarding the solution of the Entscheidungsproblem (how one can determine whether a statement is true) are Turing (1936) and Church (1936a, 1936b), but the many equivalences among their work and the computers of today were derived over subsequent decades.

read and change the data in the cell underneath it, and which possesses a property called a state; and a table of states, which give instructions for how the head should change a cell and its own state. Such instructions may take the following form: "State one: if you read a one, let it be, go right, and stay in state one. If you read a zero, change it to a one, go right, and change to state two." The innovative idea in all of this is that the data on the tape can change the state, thereby altering the instructions the machine will carry out. As already mentioned, machines of this kind are sometimes called *state machines*.

Turing initially presented only a mathematical description of such a machine and the theory behind it but eventually had a chance to build one from electric parts (see page 122). Implementing it would be fairly easy using the parts just mentioned: build a sequence of MEMORY registers, and have available one of each of the other registers (ADD, INCREMENT, and so on). Now the rules specifying the action to take in each state need to be written. For example, if the head reads a PROGRAM register set to 0, then
  —send the contents of register X to the INCREMENT register,
  —send the incremented result back to register X,
  —move the head to the next PROGRAM register.
If the head reads a PROGRAM register set to 1, then:
  —send the contents of registers X and OUT to the ADD register,
  —send the result back to register OUT,
  —move the head to the next PROGRAM register.
In short, if the head reads 0, increment X, and if it reads 1, add X to OUT. Building a machine to execute these specific operations may be difficult, but it is still just a matter of assembling a tangle of AND, OR, and NOT gates.

Once the machine is set up to perform actions contingent on register settings, then making it perform new calculations is simply a matter of resetting the PROGRAM registers to new values. To add two to a number, begin with the number in the X register, 0 in the OUT register, and 001 in the PROGRAM registers. The head first reads 0, so the machine increments the X register by 1; it then reads 0 again, so the machine again increments the X register by 1; it then reads 1, so the machine adds X to the OUT register.

Suppose the machine's operator finds an error in her notes, and needs $2x$ rather than $2 + x$. All she has to do is reset the PROGRAM registers to read 11 instead of 001; the reader may verify that this switch will leave the appropriate value in the OUT register. The fix required no new circuit diagrams and no resoldering.

And so programming is born. The computer designer writes the rules that translate from numbers in the registers to actions, such as "0 means increment register X, while 1 means add register X to register OUT." The machine is a large black box whose interface is a list of commands and whose implementation is a breadboard with a mess of vacuum tubes or transistors, cables everywhere, and a slight smell of burning. Even a mathematician who knows nothing of electrical design can work the machine by setting the memory registers appropriately, letting the machine execute its implementation, and reading the output registers after it is done.

This setup extricates a portion of the design of the logic from the design of the machine itself. The designer of the state machine still needs to solder together transistors in the right sequence for the machine to read the assembly language, but further operational instructions can be implemented by others. As explained in later chapters, the difference between this two-step process and the one-step process for implementing a purpose-specific computer allows for important legal and economic distinctions.

Modern machines work exactly like this. They have a vast array of memory registers and of specialized registers to execute certain operations. These registers are selected and built by the chip manufacturer, who patents everything as a physical device. The implementation is a physical assemblage of transistors, and the interface is a set of numbers (well, electrical signals representing numbers) that programs send to the hardware. This interface is known as the *machine code* or *assembly language.*[6]

Figure 3-1 gives some more sample translations. Although the computer can understand only two commands (0 = increment and 1 = add), it is capable of a modest amount of arithmetic. In fact, this language is already complex enough that some expressions in traditional math notation can be expressed in multiple ways. Both the program 1001 and the program 011 will leave $2X + 2$ in the OUT register.[7]

---

6. Machine code is purely hexadecimal numbers, and assembly allows pseudo-English mnemonics. The first program above in machine code would read 001, while in assembly it would be INCR, INCR, ADD. There is a nearly one-to-one correspondence between machine symbols and assembly symbols, so for the sake of the discussion here, I take them as equivalent.

7. This is related to the fact that traditional math notation has its own multiplicity of expressions: $2X + 2$ and $2(X + 1)$ mean the same thing.

**Figure 3-1. An Assembly Language and a Symbol Table**

| The language | Some translations (a symbol table) | | |
|---|---|---|---|
| 0 = Increment register X | $x + 1$ | 01 | |
| 1 = Add register X to OUT | $x + 2$ | 001 | |
| | $x + 3$ | 0001 | |
| | $2x$ | 11 | |
| | $3x$ | 111 | |
| | $2x + 1$ | 101 | |
| | $2x + 2$ | 1001 | 011 |
| | $2x + 3$ | 10001 | 0101 |
| | $2x + 4$ | 100001 | 0011 |

Also notice the shift in terminology: this stream of ones and zeros constitutes a language in the standard dictionary sense of the word.[8] Children are taught the language of arithmetic in grade school just as they are taught the more traditional languages and thus know that $X + 1$ should be read as "take X, increment it, and make a note of the outcome." But they could just as easily be taught to read 01 the same way—the symbols have meaning even without a language-specific machine to execute the instructions. It just so happens that this language can be "understood" or processed by an appropriately designed machine, in that it corresponds to electrical impulses, which correspond to a sequence of register operations.

This is also the point at which the art of construction slips from engineering to mathematics. Building a machine with all of these registers is a physical process requiring a knowledge of material science, electronics, fans, solder, and logic. Using the registers requires only a knowledge of logic. The distinction will become important later: as is fairly evident, a machine that implements a language is patentable subject matter. But is the language itself patentable? Are its uses?

8. Most dictionaries provide half a dozen definitions of *language*, one of which is typically "that which a computer can interpret," but the computer language already fits more conventional definitions as well. See the *Oxford English Dictionary*: "In generalized sense: Words and the methods of combining them for the expression of thought"; and *Merriam-Webster*: "A systematic means of communicating ideas or feelings by the use of conventionalized signs, sounds, gestures, or marks having understood meanings."

## Languages

Writing a word processor program via ADD and INCREMENT registers is clearly a task beyond human ability. Programmers thus developed programming languages more akin to standard human languages. Instead of using a human-illegible address like 0x80aa4f8 to refer to a particular register, the programming language uses a word string such as my_mothers_birthday. This is just a more convenient way of saying the same thing. A *symbol table* is needed to identify equivalent forms, so when the computer encounters the expression my_mothers_birthday, it will check the symbol table to see that this symbol means register 0x80aa4f8.

Programs are available to write this symbol table, known as a *compiler* or an *interpreter*. They will also do the same translations with more complex expressions; for example, they will convert

```
if (my_mothers_birthday == today)
        printf("Send your mother a card!");
```

into the stream of instructions that the computer will need to execute the actions described: find the registers holding the two dates, move them to a register for comparison, return the result and move on to the other instructions if the result is true, and so on. In the symbol table in figure 3-1, the left column shows human-oriented symbols, and the right columns translate them to machine-oriented ones.

### Turing Completeness

In 1972 two programmers at Bell Labs wrote a language named C to implement the scheme just described—that is, to create a language that humans could work with but that would not be too difficult to translate into a computer's assembly language.[9] Now when somebody invents new hardware whose interface is a new assembly language, all one has to do is write instructions for the compiler to translate C's semantics and keywords into the new assembly language. That done, all C programs can be run on the new computer without modification: just send the particular

9. C is so named because it is the successor to the B programming language. Alas, there was no language named A; B was the successor to BCPL (Basic Combined Programming Language), which was the successor to the CPL (Combined Programming Language). Even the foundations of computing are based on other foundations.

C code to the new compiler, which will translate it into the right machine code to send electrons to the right places on this new hardware.[10]

Today virtually everything with a microprocessor has an associated C compiler, and C thus acts as the gateway between humans and machines. Just as transistors were left behind once assembly code was in place, assembly can now be left behind in favor of more human-readable languages.

But even C contains frequent references to memory addresses that many humans find confusing. It would be better to invent a language based on the specific needs and abilities of users and then find a way to get the computer to parse and execute instructions written in the human-oriented language. Doing this is a favorite pastime of the computer scientist. For example, as of September 27, 2005, the website www.99-bottles-of-beer.net gave a listing of 807 programs to print a certain drinking song, covering 715 programming languages. C helps with this: there is no need to write a compiler that converts the programming language du jour to assembly code—just write a translator to convert the new language to C, and let C's compiler do the lower-level conversion. No assembly required.

Some things are easier to say in some languages than others, and the language a programmer chooses to use will have a definite effect on the end result. The menagerie of languages subdivides into species of specialization, such as shells, which are languages well-suited to navigating among files and running programs (ash, bash, csh, ksh, zsh); languages with many features for parsing text and spitting out more text (awk, sed, Perl); and languages with features for statistical analysis (SAS, Stata, SPSS, S-PLUS, SST, GAUSS, GAMS, GRETL, MatLab, Minitab, Limdep, Octave, R, RATS). Individual categories clearly offer a choice of many languages, and it is never obvious which is best for a given task. Even before writing a single line of code, the programmer has many paths to choose from.

Having such an abundance of languages is liberating. Although not many people can be chemists, since they would need a lab full of equipment and years of specialized learning to carry out the work, anybody who puts his or her mind to it can write a novel. Word processors and typewriters are everywhere, and no specialized training is required beyond the ability to construct complete sentences. This does not mean that just

---

10. This is theoretically how it should work, but in practice, not all compilers agree on the details of the language, so *porting* code from a C compiler for one processor to a C compiler for another processor is often compared unfavorably to pulling teeth.

anybody can write a *good* novel, but the chance to try is available to all. Computer science gives the impression of being more like chemistry, an activity for the mathy crowd and the initiated, but since programming languages are so abundant and there is one designed for any given task and any given level of experience with computers, programming is actually more like novel writing: anybody who wants to give it a shot can do so.

The diversity of languages, with their specializations and idiosyncrasies, help a diverse range of people write programs. Mathematically speaking, however, computer languages are not at all diverse, since almost all are exactly equivalent to Turing's simple tape machine.[11] Formally, this equivalence comes from:

**Theorem 1:** The Church-Turing Thesis
All computable operations can be evaluated by a Turing machine.

The exact meaning of *computable* is a technical matter that I will not delve into here; roughly, it means "anything a computer could possibly do." The Church-Turing thesis states that any computer program, written in any language, can be rewritten as a Turing machine. Hence given two languages like C and Perl, if (C = a Turing machine) and (Perl = a Turing machine), then it does indeed follow that (C = Perl). That is, any program written in one language can be translated to any other. In the terminology of mathematicians, making the translation from one Turing complete language to another is *trivial*—it may take Herculean effort, but it is an entirely mechanical exercise. All languages that are equivalent to Turing's specification are said to be *Turing complete*.

Turing completeness is a surprisingly low bar. Many hand calculators can understand a Turing complete language. PDF (Portable Document Format), in which many documents on the Internet are available, is itself a Turing complete language. Word processors such as Microsoft Word or Sun's StarOffice typically include their own Turing complete language.

Church's contribution to the Church-Turing thesis was a means of writing equations, known as the *lambda calculus*, which is equivalent to Turing's tape machine. That is, he discovered a method of pure mathematical expression that has been shown to be Turing complete. Programs in C, Perl, and the others mentioned earlier are therefore equivalent to a system of lambda calculus equations: it may be a laborious exercise, but

---

11. A few specialized languages—such as the C preprocessor, sed, and most markup languages—do not bother to be Turing complete.

one could construct a symbol table with Perl expressions on the left and equations in the lambda calculus on the right.[12] This point will prove to be important in a legal context, when courts try to draw a line between pure mathematics and software. Since any program in any Turing complete programming language is identical to a system of equations in the lambda calculus, the courts will be unable to draw such a line.

## The Nouns and Verbs of a Language

To reiterate, a programming language is a means of communicating instructions to a computer. These instructions are formal rules that make it possible to specify what data a computer will act upon and what actions to take under various conditions. The data and data structures acted upon can be considered the nouns of the language and the functions the verbs.

### Data Structures

Data structures are simply a list of small pieces of data amalgamated to describe something complex. A standard structure for representing an individual, for example, might contain slots for the person's name, age, and social security number:

```
struct person{
char * name;
int age;
long int social_security_number;
struct person * next; //(See below.)
}
```

Designing a data structure to describe one person is easy, but doing so for hundreds of people produces new difficulties. A few solutions to the problem are suggested by the way a deli handles a crowd of customers. One is to have everyone stand in line, so that the people physically represent the conceptual order in which they will be served. Alternatively, if

---

12. Barring some details, here is the symbol table converting the "0 = increment, 1 = add" language to the lambda calculus:

0    $(\lambda \text{ x x+1}) \text{ X}$
1    $(\lambda \text{ x } \lambda \text{ y x + y}) \text{ X OUT.}$

Adam knows Beth comes after him, and Beth knows that Carl comes after her, then there is no need for them to actually stand in line. Beth could wander off to the bread aisle as long as Adam comes and taps her when he is done.

Returning to the hard drive, the first, linear method of organizing low-level data into high-level structures is known as an array. It is easy to implement, although problems can arise, particularly when the space set aside for the line is too small to hold the number of people who arrive. The second method is a linked list. Notice the next entry in the person structure above: this is where Adam would keep a pointer to Beth and Beth would keep a pointer to Carl.

The data on computer memory with an array look very different from those on a drive with a linked list. The person structure is 16 bytes long on the typical personal computer, so an array of a million persons would be a single 16,000,000-byte block somewhere in memory. The linked list could have persons scattered all over the computer's memory—maybe even on different computers entirely. Provided the pointers are all correctly maintained, the even-numbered structures could be on a computer in Delaware and the odd-numbered ones in Utah.

Or, one can give up on the idea of a line entirely, and have each person point to two or three successors, producing a tree structure with one root person, who points to two successors, next_left and next_right, who each point to two successors of their own, and so on. There are dozens of ways to grow and prune trees as more people come along, the relative merits of which are the subject of many a Ph.D. dissertation in computer science. As noted in chapter 4, some argue that since concepts such as sorting rules are used to shunt physical objects, be they people or magnetic pulses, they can be patented.

A word processor's documents provide another example of a data structure. Like the persons in the structure examined earlier, a document is a representation in the computer's memory of a certain aggregation of data (in this case, a paper or a letter). The data structure of a word processor's documents typically includes fields for the name of the author, the date of creation, and other characteristics, along with a list of all of the text in the document; the machine dumps this structure to the hard drive when the document is saved. Some programs make no distinction between the data structure saved to the hard drive and the data structure that the program uses when editing, whereas others have a different format on disk. The latest trend has been to use the human-readable extensible markup language (XML) to format the data written to a file. Regardless of the format, the files saved by a computer are just another data structure, albeit one that continues to exist after the program closes, and that can be e-mailed, archived, and carried from computer to computer.

Suppose that an especially fastidious programmer wants to write a database program that will pull out the names of people who owe him money and will prepare nicely formatted letters to this effect in Microsoft Word. The programmer would have to know Word's document data structure precisely in order to write something that Word would understand to be a set of business letters. The file format is thus a part of the interface between the program and other software that programmers need to interact with Word in productive ways. Microsoft, hoping to retain some control of what programs could interface with its word processor, kept the file format a badly guarded secret.

Indeed, every document saved provided a clue to the format, so engineers working for competitors were able to work backwards to determine what Word was doing. In response, Microsoft kept changing the file format. Patents would solve this pesky problem for Microsoft: if the company could patent the Word document structure, and a competitor learned the format and wrote a program that interoperates with it, then rather than tweaking the format again, Microsoft could simply sue the competitor. Microsoft has applied for a patent for its Word document format in the United States and the European Union.[13] Figure 3-2 shows the claimed system for reading its XML format—the text gives minimal elaboration beyond this. Clearly, any word processor that can read Microsoft's claimed document format would be covered. The issue is discussed further in chapter 7.

A data structure can be nontrivial, reaching into the farthest depths of pure computer science research. But in the end, it is a method of organizing data—a sorting scheme and nothing more. U.S. patent guidelines disallow patents on data structures, unless they are written onto a computer-readable medium.[14] This would encompass any data structure with an appropriately worded patent application. Outside of patents, there are

---

13. U.S. patent application 20040210818, "Word-processing document stored in a single XML file that may be manipulated by applications that understand XML"; European patent application 03009719.0, available as EP publication EP 1 376 387 A2.
14. MPEP 2106 IV B 1 (a).

Figure 3-2.  Microsoft's Patent Application for Programs That Read Word Documents: Claims 17, 18, and 19

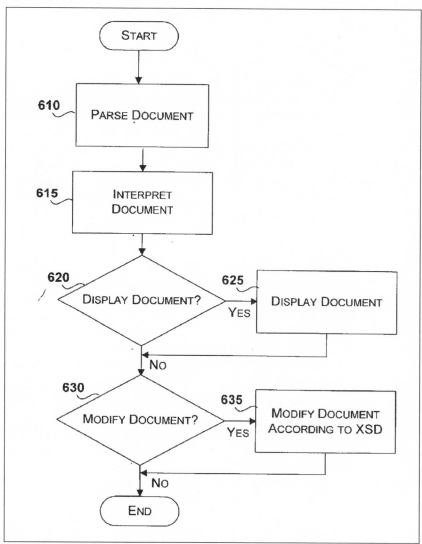

two other means by which the author of a data structure may claim exclusive rights to its use, also discussed in chapter 7.

### Functions

The verbs, or *functions*, of programming languages are lists of instructions in a neat black box. Like the black boxes above, it is described by a list of items that must be put into the box, a statement of what the box will spit out, and a list of steps that the machine will take to go from inputs to output. A function to find somebody in a linked list is shown in figure 3-3.

This example shows how functions can also be broken down into an implementation and an interface. To modify the function in figure 3-3, one would need to have the implementation in hand, but a user who only wanted to use the function in other matters would need only the interface, which is summarized in the top lines:

```
struct person * find_person (char *name_sought);
/* Find the person in the list whose name matches
   name_sought */
```

This indicates that if a programmer calls `find_person("Steve")`, the function will return the `person` structure representing Steve.

The true joy of the function system is that once a black box like `find_person` is working and sealed off, it can be used to build bigger, more complex black boxes. That is, given the interface, functions at a higher level can call other functions at a lower level.

Suppose that a coder needs to print the weight/height ratio of everyone on a list. Here are the ingredients required to complete this task: a function to look up the height and weight assigned to a name, a function to calculate the ratio, and a function to print the results. Each of these functions is small enough that it would be trivial to write them using any common programming language. It would also be trivial to chain them together into a function that reads the list and prints the weight/height ratios.

The result is not unlike a Rube Goldberg machine: the main function calls the listing function, which calls the search function, which calls the step-through-the-list function, which may call who-knows-what internally, and those internals will send electrons to certain registers on the computer's processor. At the end of that entire procedure, the ratio-calculator function starts, calling up its own tower of subfunctions; and

**Figure 3-3.  One Doesn't Need to Understand the Internals
of a Black Box to Use It**

```
struct person *find_person(char *name_sought){
/* find the person in the list whose name matches name_sought */
    struct person *tr=first_person;      //start at the list's head
    while(strcmp(tr->name,name_sought))  //If tr's name doesn't match
        tr = tr->next;                   //move on to the next name.
    return tr;                           //If it does match, return tr.
}
```

finally the print function begins another stack of instructions. As impossible as it may be to trace through the whole system, each part, on its own scale, is easy to write and understand.

Typically, functions that are useful for a given purpose are bundled into *function libraries*.[15] For example, a linked list library would include functions to initialize a list, add and delete nodes, and search for entries. Given this bundle of functions and an interface explaining their use, the programmer need not spend a moment thinking about how the list is implemented, whether pointers are valid, and so on. Having pulled data from the list, the functions in a font library will render it on the screen in a pleasing way, without requiring the programmer to know anything about kerning or rasterization. On the input side, a mouse pointer library can interpret the user's button clicks, assuming the programmer has found a library to draw buttons on the screen.

To write a word processor or spreadsheet, the programmer now only needs to find the right toolboxes and then chain the tools together to produce the final product. As with the lower-level tasks, the process is both trivial to do and very difficult to do well.

Again, those who need to draw from these libraries in their own work will have no interest in the details of implementation, so the implementation is typically hidden. The most common means of hiding it is to convert the file containing the human-readable source code to object code

15. Most libraries declare a number of structures on which the functions operate. Nevertheless, the common custom is to refer to these aggregates of predefined nouns and verbs as function libraries. In some schools of programming, the functions are bound inside data structures, in which case the bundle is called an *object library*.

(the stream of hexademical machine language that the compiler spits out) and leave the interface in the original pseudo-English programming language. This setup is fine for programmers who will use the function because cognitive effort is limited, so just knowing how to interface with the function is exactly as much as the average programmer cares to know.

From a legal perspective, this is a delicate split. The designer of the library may not want others copying his or her functions, but the implementation has to be public and is a strong hint as to the internals of the black box. The story of software intellectual property is filled with people who run across a new interface to a new black box and then build a black box to work just like the original. Whether they have a right to do so is one of the key questions explored in this book.

What about the web browsers, word processors, and other everyday programs? They are simply function libraries. Like the other equivalencies in this chapter, this is not a metaphorical one: each program includes a single function named `main` that auto-executes when the program is started; that function calls a function to render a window on the screen, and a function to draw toolbars, and a function to wait for user input, and a thousand other functions to implement the interface users are familiar with. Users then ask the program to call more functions; for example, a Microsoft Word user may click on the File menu and then the Save item, or may directly call Word's `ActiveDocument.Save` function. Apart from the fact that a function named `main` will be automatically called when the program starts, the word processing program's internals are exactly like any other function library.

By now, the programmer will be awash in equivalent means of getting the computer to shunt its electrons. Commands can be issued in C, Perl, FORTRAN, or Lisp, and for any one language there are infinite ways to write a single function. Or if one is lazy, one can search for a specific function from existing function libraries and then write a program to call the function, by a typed command or a mouse-click or by calling it automatically when the program starts. The function could use any of a vast array (or a vast list, or a vast tree) of data structures for its internal bookkeeping.

Alternatively, the story can be cast in terms of symbol tables defining a language: since a function call expands to the function's internals, one could write a symbol table with the call on the left and the expansion on the right. One such table already in existence contains a word processor's interface on the left and VisualBasic code on the right; another has

VisualBasic code on the left and C language on the right; yet another, C on the left and equations in the lambda calculus on the right. By chaining all these symbol tables together, one would be able to express the word processor as the pure mathematical algorithm it embodies.

Given a computable task, any two competent programmers could write a program to perform the task. The process is trivial: if the task is too difficult, break it down into smaller parts, write those subfunctions, and when enough subfunctions are completed, the main function will be easy. In view of the astounding number of choices available in such an exercise, the two programmers' solutions could be vastly different. One might be more appropriate for large data sets, the other for small sets; one might have a point-and-click interface and the other a command-line interface. The find_person function in figure 3-2 is a valid means of writing such a function, but it will crash if the list is empty or the name is not found; one programmer may be careful to consider these contingencies and the other may miss a detail.

At the same time, the two solutions are reasonably likely to have much in common. Run the first programmer's FORTRAN code through an automatic translator like f2c, and it may wind up looking very much like the second programmer's C code. An appropriately abstract flowchart representation of the two solutions may be entirely identical.

The stage is now set for the battles over intellectual property. There is abundant room for independent creativity and solving problems in new ways, but at the right level of abstraction, all of these unique methods may wash into the same flowchart, which is merely another representation of an equation. The layers of a program outnumber those of even the thickest onions. Hence the fundamental economic question about software patents—how broad should their scope be?—could potentially be answered by setting intellectual property protections at any of a number of levels, such as the flowchart level, the source code level, or the level of the physical state machine. Chapter 4 looks at judicial opinion on this question.

# CHAPTER FOUR

# Patenting Math

Imagine a continuous line of inventions, with physical machines built from transistors and diodes at one end and pure mathematics at the other end. Any given piece of software falls somewhere along this spectrum. The line between the patentable and unpatentable items along this continuum should meet three basic criteria: physical machines should be patentable subject matter, pure mathematics should not, and whatever distinction is made between the two categories should be clear and unambiguous.

Software may not fit the U.S. Code's definition of patentable subject matter for two main reasons. The first is that software is math, and it is universally agreed that pure mathematics cannot be patented. The second is that software has no physical manifestation beyond symbols on paper or bits on a hard drive, whereas it is generally assumed that patents apply to the manipulation of physical objects. In its first rulings on the subject—*Gottschalk* v. *Benson* (1972) and *Parker* v. *Flook* (1978)—the U.S. Supreme Court endorsed both arguments, thus ruling that the patentability line should be drawn at physical machines only.

The turning point for the physical manifestation question came in *Diamond* v. *Diehr* (1981), a case about a rubber-curing machine with a significant amount of software. The Supreme Court ruled that this invention was indeed patentable because of its physical manifestation—the patentability line was moved to inventions with a physical component of any kind. In the wake of this decision, the number of software patent applications to the U.S. Patent and Trademark Office (USPTO) using some sort of physical terminology increased: instead of claiming "a method to calculate," applicants claimed "a general-purpose computer on which is programmed a method to calculate." Some of these technically physical inventions were granted patents, and some were not.

The Court of Appeals for the Federal Circuit (CAFC) convened to clarify the issue and in *In re Alappat* (1994) ruled that these rewordings made the invention a physical device. In fact, if the author of the patent was a little careless and forgot to use the right wording, the patent examiner was obliged to insert the correct terms.

Then in *State Street* v. *Signature* (1998), the CAFC drew the current line regarding subject matter: a pure mathematical algorithm may not be patentable, but when it has any useful application, it becomes patentable. This means that if applicants assign real-world names to the variables in their equations, they meet the requirement. Even this line has not held, and many patents do not even bother to disguise their mathematical algorithms with a real-world application.

## Loopholes

Many patent advocates believe that mere technicalities about form should not prevent an applicant from getting a patent. The CAFC, some say, is stocked with pro-patent judges who wrote these rulings to simply close the technical loopholes that kept software from the patents it deserves.[1] The change of wording may look like a silly trick, but it is intended to shut down what the judges seemed to feel was a silly objection to begin with.

However, the objection is not simply a technicality. Because it is difficult or impossible to distinguish between applied and pure math, patent rules that allow applied math send the law down a slippery slope with the patenting of abstract mathematical procedures at its end.

The physical manifestation rule, defined appropriately, could be an excellent way to draw the line. The courts were unable or unwilling to distinguish between what most would consider a clear physical manifestation (like a rubber-curing machine) and a trivial physical manifestation (like writing to a hard drive); the ambiguity of the line again led to

---

1. On the CAFC being stocked with pro-patent judges, see Jaffe and Lerner (2004, p. 105).

patentable math. However, the state machine and the states into which that machine can be placed are easy to distinguish, and drawing the patentability line between the two makes machines patentable, leaves math unpatentable, and depends on objective standards rather than judgment calls.

## Math

All the arguments about fostering innovation still apply to mathematics. The best theorems are those that a mathematician spends months working on, tirelessly trying possibilities and dead ends until finally reaching a conclusion. When other mathematicians see the result properly framed and explained, they exclaim, "That's obvious!" and run to their offices to apply the result as if it were their own. In a field where jobs and funding are limited, giving mathematicians exclusive domain over the results they toiled over would provide a valuable incentive for them to work hard.

But it has been unequivocally agreed throughout legislative and judicial history that a mathematical equation is not patentable.[2] The strictly economic reasons will appear below—but on top of economic efficiency, mathematics is seen as a collection of laws of nature, which no person may have domain over.

Thomas Jefferson, in a classic letter to a colleague, reasoned that allowing patents on pure ideas makes no sense:

> It would be curious then, if an idea, the fugitive fermentation of an individual brain, could, of natural right, be claimed in exclusive and stable property. If nature has made any one thing less susceptible than all others of exclusive property, it is the action of the thinking power called an idea, which an individual may exclusively possess as long as he keeps it to himself; but the moment it is divulged, it forces itself into the possession of every one, and the receiver cannot dispossess himself of it. Its peculiar character, too, is that no one possesses the less, because every other possesses the whole of it. He who receives an idea from me, receives instruction himself without lessening mine; as he who lights his taper at mine, receives light without darkening me. That ideas should freely spread from one to another over the globe, for the moral and

---

2. All five of the major decisions discussed in this chapter cede this fact at some point.

mutual instruction of man, and improvement of his condition, seems to have been peculiarly and benevolently designed by nature, when she made them, like fire, expansible over all space, without lessening their density in any point, and like the air in which we breathe, move, and have our physical being, incapable of confinement or exclusive appropriation.[3]

Throughout U.S. history, the courts have taken mathematical equations to be pure ideas and, following Jefferson, concluded that as such they should not be patentable.

### For the Pragmatists

Some readers may not be concerned about the metaphysics of owning ideas and simply want to know whether letting people patent mathematical ideas would make for a better or worse economy. For those readers, I offer a laundry list of reasons for leaving theoretical math in the public domain. It is worth noting that if we replace "mathematical result" with "software," all of the arguments presented in this section would still hold.

Independent invention is very common in both mathematics and computer science. The theorem central to this book is an example: Church and Turing independently derived the components of what is now called the Church-Turing thesis in the same year. Because independent invention is not a defense against patent infringement claims, any such hyphenated theorem would be a lawsuit in the making. One reason for the frequency of simultaneous invention is that equipment requirements are almost nil, so any mathematician in the world could be working on any given problem right now. The history of mathematics is filled with impoverished geniuses who lived in countries such as colonial-era India or Spain in the Middle Ages. Imagine the effect if all such people had to purchase licenses from patent owners before embarking on a project.

Just as computer science raises an infinite tower of turtles, all mathematics (save for a sliver of basic results) builds upon other mathematics.[4] A new result generally consists of a series of preexisting definitions and the application of a series of past results; an especially long proof may draw on a dozen or more established theorems, and a complete book on one topic could use hundreds. Obtaining permission from their many

3. Thomas Jefferson, letter to Isaac MacPherson (August 13, 1813).
4. This is no coincidence: the system of attacking a programming problem—encapsulating problems into subproblems and reducing problems to other previously solved problems—is a direct imitation of common methods of proving mathematical theorems.

authors would create paralyzing levels of expense and paperwork. (This is an application of Coase's theorem, discussed in chapter 5.)

A patent on a good algorithm would surely make a few mathematicians exceptionally wealthy—but where would the money come from? Most of the profits made by a wealthy theorem-owner would come from other mathematicians, so patents would not make the industry as a whole richer or better funded. Money would simply change hands. Of course, patents used by biologists, chemists, or other applied mathematicians would feed money into the theoretical math industry, but since the primary consumers of mathematical theorems are other mathematicians, this profit would likely be small in relation to the amount of money churning about within the theoretical math industry itself.

For all of these reasons, patents on mathematical algorithms do not make economic sense. The theoretical math industry would make some more money from outside sources, but at the cost of drastic reductions in efficiency within itself and new barriers to entry in a field famous for its relatively low entry costs.

## Mathematical Utility

The biggest problem with patenting a math procedure is its immense breadth. Although it is the joy of abstraction that the same equation can be used to describe hundreds of specific applications, in the context of patents this becomes a pain: anyone who writes a program that follows the steps of the algorithm involved would be infringing, regardless of the genre of the application. The courts have tried to draw a wedge between the abstract equation and the application, but it has not held because mathematicians and computer scientists make no distinction.

In a seminal paper on matching sets of actors, two economists, David Gale and Lloyd S. Shapley, describe what is called the "marriage algorithm."[5] The application easiest to envision matches boys to girls, but the same algorithm can be (and in some places is) used to match students to schools, or to carry out any other two-sided matching.

Without discussing the algorithm in detail, it is interesting to consider how the two mathematicians view their own work: "In making the special assumptions needed in order to analyze our problem mathematically,

5. Gale and Shapley (1962).

we necessarily moved further away from the original college admission question, and eventually in discussing the marriage problem, we abandoned reality altogether and entered the world of mathematical make-believe." Of course, Gale and Shapley's abstract results are then applied directly to real-world situations like employees matching to employers, and the language of their paper alternates between abstract and real-world descriptions.

### A Combinatorial Optimization Problem

To give another example, one of the most salient questions in mathematics today is this:

Let $C$ be a set of $N$ points in a space endowed with a metric $D(\cdot,\cdot)$. What is the ordered sequence of $C$, $\{c_1, c_2, \ldots, c_n\}$ that minimizes

$$\left[\sum_{i=1}^{n-1} D(C_i, C_{i+1})\right] + D(C_n, C_1)?$$

This is commonly known as the traveling salesman problem: what is the shortest route that will allow a salesman to visit a given set of cities? But if $C$ is a collection of networked computers and $D$ is the time it takes for a packet of data to travel from one computer to another, the same symbols become a model of Internet traffic routing. Or if $C$ is a list of airports, this becomes a problem of designing flight schedules. Consequently, giving an airline a patent on the algorithm it uses to calculate the shortest distance for a flight route could raise the cost of research on speeding up Internet traffic. Requiring that a patentable item have a specific purpose does not solve the problem because a creative attorney could simply draft a patent that covers both cases—or just apply for two patents.

Some nonmathematicians (such as certain judges) believe mathematics research consists first of purely abstract work, then of applying the *deus ex machina* results in the concrete world. The actual process is a constant mix of the ethereal and ephemeral.

### Algorithms

Although most of what students learn in algebra class consists simply of equations, mathematicians normally think in algorithms. For example, the traveling salesman problem is not really "What is the shortest route given a set of cities $C$?" but "If you gave me any set of cities, what steps would I take to derive the shortest route?" The solution would be some sort of flowchart showing the series of calculations one would need to go from a set $C$ to an efficient route. As Gale and Shapley point out, it is a mistake to think mathematicians spend their days writing down systems of equations:

> Our result provides a handy counterexample to some of the stereotypes which non-mathematicians believe mathematics to be concerned with.
>
> Most mathematicians at one time or another have probably found themselves in the position of trying to refute the notion that they are people with "a head for figures," or that they "know a lot of formulas." At such times it may be convenient to have an illustration at hand to show that mathematics need not be concerned with figures, either numerical or geometrical. For this purpose we recommend the statement and proof of our [marriage algorithm results]. The argument is carried out not in mathematical symbols but in ordinary English; there are no obscure or technical terms. Knowledge of calculus is not presupposed. In fact, one hardly needs to know how to count. Yet any mathematician will immediately recognize the argument as mathematical.[6]

The mathematics in question is not a system of equations, but a series of steps to a conclusion—an algorithm. Of course, patents on physical entities include their share of algorithms, such as patent 6,905,665 for a "Method for purifying carbon monoxide," or patent 5,484,378 for a "Sheet-folding method." The key difference between these algorithms and those embodied in software lies in the Church-Turing thesis. There is a direct, trivial translation between the algorithm in a piece of software and an equation in the lambda calculus, or between Gale and Shapley's marriage algorithm and another lambda calculus equation.[7] So even those who ignore Gale and Shapley's point that mathematics is about algorithms and not equations must still concede that the flowcharts of the average software patent are merely a more human-readable translation of a pure mathematical formula. This is true of physical processes only in a

6. Gale and Shapley (1962, p. 15).
7. Also, do not forget the Curry-Howard isomorphism, which states that there is a one-to-one mapping between programs and deductive mathematical proofs.

metaphorical sense and is why the rulings that ushered software patents into existence do not rely on comparison to process patents.

Gale and Shapley conclude, "What, then, to raise the old question once more, is mathematics? The answer, it appears, is that any argument which is carried out with sufficient precision is mathematical."[8] It is no mere coincidence that Gale and Shapley's definition of mathematics—an argument carried out with sufficient precision—also works perfectly as a definition of computer code.

## Congress Passes the Buck

When Thomas Jefferson wrote the first Patent Act in 1793, it included a single sentence explaining what may be patented. The patent law was revised in 1836, 1870, 1874, and 1952, and over the course of these centuries of revision, the Congress changed only one word of Jefferson's text, replacing "art" with "process."[9] Here is the current form:

> 35 U.S.C. §101. – Inventions patentable
> Whoever invents or discovers any new and useful process, machine, manufacture, or composition of matter, or any new and useful improvement thereof, may obtain a patent therefor, subject to the conditions and requirements of this title.

The code now includes a bit more detail about who can file (§102), what is "obvious" in the biotech context (§103), and how inventions discovered or used on U.S. spaceships are subject to U.S. patent law (§105). But as far as the patentability of software is concerned, it comes under the succinct law crafted by Jefferson. This may suggest that the law has been entirely stagnant. In more than 200 years, after revolutionary developments in, among other things, internal combustion, electricity, and electronics, Congress managed to change only one word.

But the way the law is interpreted has been dynamically changing. The courts have modified their interpretations of the law to suit the needs of the times. For example, when Samuel F. B. Morse filed patent 1,647 for an "Improvement in the mode of communicating information by signals by

---

8. Gale and Shapley (1962, p. 15).

9. For a good summary of the history of patent law, see *Diamond* v. *Chakrabarty*, 447 U.S. 303 (1980).

the application of electro-magnetism," he claimed not only his telegraph and eponymous code, but *any* means of transmitting data via electricity:

> Eighth [claim]. I do not propose to limit myself to the specific machinery or parts of machinery described in the foregoing specification and claims; the essence of my invention being the use of the motive power of the electric or galvanic current, which I call electro-magnetism, however developed for marking or printing intelligible characters, signs, or letters, at any distances, being a new application of that power of which I claim to be the first inventor or discoverer.[10]

Morse's claim seems to fit what is now §101 closely enough for the patent to have been granted, and one could make a fighting argument that he was the inventor of the concept of telecommunications. But the Supreme Court saw that a flood of new inventions would be forthcoming in the field:

> For aught that we now know some future inventor, in the onward march of science, may discover a mode of writing or printing at a distance by means of the electric or galvanic current, without using any part of the process or combination set forth in the plaintiff's specification. His invention may be less complicated—less liable to get out of order—less expensive in construction, and in its operation. But yet if it is covered by this patent the inventor could not use it, nor the public have the benefit of it without the permission of this patentee.[11]

Congress did not have to change its law to accommodate the birth of telecommunications, because the courts interpreted the law to maximize the potential for progress in the new field. One could argue that court interpretation of patent law has changed in every generation to accommodate changes in technology.

If modern courts maintained such a responsibility toward a fair interpretation of patents in the new technology of software, then Congress would be justified in its continued steady support of Jefferson's words.

---

10. The patent was reissued twice, and the wording here, which the Supreme Court ruled upon, is from later revisions.
11. *O'Reilly v. Morse*, 56 U.S. (15 How.) 62 (1853).

Since the 1970s, both the Supreme Court and the CAFC have made key rulings about whether to revisit patent law to accommodate the fundamental differences between state machines and states. First, the Supreme Court, in a trilogy of rulings between 1972 and 1981, showed due circumspection in the face of a technological revolution. These rulings can be used to characterize a consistent view that a mathematical algorithm by itself is not patentable, but when extended via an innovative physical device, the aggregate machine is. Subsequent rulings by the CAFC, however, vehemently rejected the conclusion that patent law should make any distinction between software and steam engines.

## The Supreme Court Draws the Line

Among the three key software patents ruled upon by the Supreme Court, two were struck down and one was granted, indicating that the Court did not see the inclusion of software as grounds for rejecting a patent but also did not believe that equations, however practical or baroque, could be treated like any other new design.

### Gottschalk v. Benson

The complaint raised in *Gottschalk* v. *Benson* was that since pure math is not patentable, software that does little beyond restating pure math should not be patentable either. The claimed patent was for a method to convert from one system of writing binary numbers to another.[12] The court ruled that since this was a purely mathematical exercise and the patent would preclude any use of the mathematical formula, it was not patentable subject matter. The 1972 decision stated:

> It is conceded that one may not patent an idea. But in practical effect that would be the result if the formula for converting BCD [binary-coded decimal] numerals to pure binary numerals were patented in this case. The mathematical formula involved here has no substantial practical application except in connection with a digital computer,

12. There are a few ways to convert a number like 36 to a binary form. One (binary-coded decimal) method would be to convert the number 3 to binary, 011, and then the number 6, which would be 110, and concatenate the two to 011110. Another (plain old binary) method would be to convert the number 36 all at once: 100100.

which means that if the judgment below is affirmed, the patent would wholly pre-empt the mathematical formula and in practical effect would be a patent on the algorithm itself.[13]

In short, the invention was nothing but a broad mathematical idea and therefore not patentable.

### Parker v. Flook

Six years later, the Court buttressed the case against software patents by ruling in *Parker* v. *Flook* that not only was a mathematical formula not patentable but adding a simple physical device to a mathematical formula did not justify a patent.[14] The case was about the validity of a patent claim for a device that would conduct certain measurements (mostly of the temperature and pressure of hydrocarbons), use the measurements in a few calculations, and ring an alarm if a certain variable passed a specific limit. The Supreme Court ruled that adding a single bell or whistle to a mathematical formula is not sufficient to make the entire apparatus patentable:

> The notion that post-solution activity, no matter how conventional or obvious in itself, can transform an unpatentable principle into a patentable process exalts form over substance. A competent drafts-man could attach some form of post-solution activity to almost any mathematical formula; the Pythagorean Theorem would not have been patentable, or partially patentable, because a patent application contained a final step indicating that the formula, when solved, could be usefully applied to existing surveying techniques.

In Flook's invention, the mathematical formula was applied to a specific purpose of real human utility. However, the Court reasoned that this was not a sufficiently novel and nonobvious extension of the mathematical formula to qualify as a patentable invention in its entirety. In other words, all of the novelty to the invention was in a piece of nonpatentable mathematics, and the application of that piece of math to the real world displayed no ingenuity.

13. 409 U.S. 63 (1972).
14. 437 U.S. 584 (1978).

## Diamond v. Diehr

James Diehr and Theodore Lutton of the Federal-Mogul Corporation held a patent on a process for controlling rubber-molding presses by computer. Essentially, their system measured the temperature of rubber in a mold and fed that information, as well as data on the elapsed time, to a computer. From these data the computer calculated the time required for the rubber to cure and at the end of that time signaled for the mold to be opened. This procedure involves a great deal of software and math, but also industrial equipment. The court ruled that the formula by itself was not patentable, but the machine as a whole was patentable subject matter:

> We view respondents' claims as nothing more than a process for molding rubber products and not as an attempt to patent a mathematical formula. We recognize, of course, that when a claim recites a mathematical formula (or scientific principle or phenomenon of nature), an inquiry must be made into whether the claim is seeking patent protection for that formula in the abstract. A mathematical formula as such is not accorded the protection of our patent laws, *Gottschalk* v. *Benson*, . . . and this principle cannot be circumvented by attempting to limit the use of the formula to a particular technological environment, *Parker* v. *Flook*. . . . Similarly, insignificant postsolution activity will not transform . . . an unpatentable principle into a patentable process. . . . To hold otherwise would allow a competent draftsman to evade the recognized limitations on the type of subject matter eligible for patent protection. On the other hand, when a claim containing a mathematical formula implements or applies that formula in a structure or process which, when considered as a whole, is performing a function which the patent laws were designed to protect (e.g., transforming or reducing an article to a different state or thing), then the claim satisfies the requirements of [35 U.S. Code §] 101. Because we do not view respondents' claims as an attempt to patent a mathematical formula, but rather to be drawn to an industrial process . . . for the molding of rubber products, we affirm the judgment of the Court of Customs and Patent Appeals.
>
> It is so ordered.[15]

15. 450 U.S. 175 (1981).

This ruling respects the concept of mathematics as a law of nature. Many physical machines make extensive use of gravity as one step in the larger machine's working but do not of course claim gravity as the author's sole property, nor does the use of gravity in one step out of many preclude the entire machine from being patentable. Similarly, the presence of an algorithm or mathematical equation in an invention does not invalidate the patent if it is one step of many, but if there is nothing to the invention but an equation, then there is nothing to be patented.

## The CAFC Closes the Loopholes and Opens the Floodgates

In *Diamond* v. *Diehr* the court concluded that some machinery is necessary for patentability, but this raised another key question without providing an answer: *how much* additional machinery would be required to make a new algorithm patentable? One could reconcile the above rulings by saying that the physical component of the invention must be novel and nonobvious, so adding a simple alarm is not sufficient, whereas an inventive rubber-curing machine is. This would mean that a nontrivial amount of inventiveness must be present on the physical end of the process.

However, many have answered the question much more broadly. In three penecontemporaneous rulings, the U.S. district courts (which heard patent appeals during this period) established the Freeman-Walter-Abele test, which asks of a patent application that recites an algorithm whether the overall invention includes more than just the algorithm; if so, then the overall device would be patentable.[16] Many took this test to mean that *any* physical manifestation of the algorithm was patentable if the machine as a whole (algorithm plus parts) was inventive.[17] One could argue that using stock parts in a creative way is still inventive, whether those stock parts are wires and transistors or a ready-built Turing machine. Thus instead of claiming a patent on "an algorithm to . . ." inventors could claim a patent on "a general-purpose computer on which is loaded an algorithm to. . . ."

---

16. *In re Freeman,* 573 F.2d 1237 (1978); *In re Walter,* 618 F.2d 758 (1980); *In re Abele,* 684 F.2d 902 (1982).
17. Merges, Menell, and Lemley (2000).

## In re Alappat

These claims came under scrutiny in 1994. At that time, the USPTO was accepting some applications for "a general-purpose computer on which is loaded an algorithm to . . ." and rejecting others. The CAFC then convened a panel to decide whether such patents should be accepted or rejected. The test case, *In re Alappat,* centered on a rasterizer for oscilloscope screens (a software-based system for smoothing potentially jagged waveforms prior to display). In upholding the patent, the CAFC panel explained: "We have held that such programming creates a new machine, because a general purpose computer in effect becomes a special purpose computer once it is programmed to perform particular functions pursuant to instructions from program software."[18] They thus accepted the new wording: the computer running the software is a physical machine, so it is patentable subject matter in the traditional sense.

In fact, the court took *Diamond* v. *Diehr* a step further to make it still easier for software to be patented. It applied 35 U.S.C. §112, paragraph 6, which says that if a patent applicant describes an algorithmic step for executing some function without explicitly stating what materials should be used, then the patent examiner should read the patent as if the materials were explicitly listed.[19] In the situation here, the court ruled this to mean that if the draftsman forgot to prefix "a general-purpose computer on which is loaded" to his or her claim for an algorithm, then the examiner must read the claim as if that clause were in place. To borrow the words of the *Diamond* v. *Diehr* ruling, not only could "a competent draftsman . . . evade the recognized limitations on the type of subject matter eligible for patent protection," but an incompetent one could, too.

This rewording trick extends beyond algorithms. The successor to *In re Alappat, In re Lowry,* established that a hard disk on which a data structure is written is a substantially different hard disk from one without a data structure; thus "a data structure to store information" is not

---

18. 33 F.3d 1526 (1994).

19. "An element in a claim for a combination may be expressed as a means or step for performing a specified function without the recital of structure, material, or acts in support thereof, and such claim shall be construed to cover the corresponding structure, material, or acts described in the specification and equivalents thereof."

patentable, but "a hard disk or computer memory on which is encoded a data structure to store information" is patentable.[20]

These rulings suggest that the court found the physical/nonphysical distinction to be fictitious. After all, Jefferson and two centuries of Congresses did not use the word "physical" in 35 U.S.C. §101, and there is no reason to read that word into their code. The wording trick was the CAFC's means of shutting down complaints about physical versus informational technology.[21]

Notice that these rulings rely heavily on the claim that a machine with a program is a new physical device, because the process the algorithm executes is pure math. Some modern advocates of software patents compare software to other processes that operate on common objects in a creative manner, but as noted earlier, a sheet-folding algorithm has a mathematical equivalent only in a metaphorical sense, while all software is literally equivalent to a pure mathematical equation. Judge Rich, the author of the *In re Alappat* decision, concedes that by itself, a mathematical algorithm—a process codified in software—is not patentable subject matter. But he rules that that is the incorrect perspective: instead, it is the "new machine" created by the programming of a purely mathematical algorithm on a physical device that is patentable subject matter.

### State Street Bank & Trust v. Signature Financial Group

The *Alappat* decision does not cover any physical encoding of information. For example, if a song is put on a compact disc, the disc still cannot be patented, even though it is a physical device that provides the practical benefit of producing pleasing sounds. As the *Manual of Patent Examining Procedure (MPEP)* explains, "Such a result would exalt form over substance."[22]

The most commonly cited case that sets the rule as to what algorithms may be patented when written to a hard drive is *State Street Bank & Trust v. Signature Financial Group*.[23] This case was about a patent for a series of flowcharts that described the accounting necessary to maintain a

20. 32 F.3d 1579 (1994).
21. Judge Giles Rich (1904–99) was the author of both the *In re Alappat* and *State Street* rulings discussed extensively in this chapter. There is every reason to believe that he knew Congress's intent when writing the patent statutes, because he himself drafted the Patent Act of 1952, upon which modern patent law is based.
22. *MPEP* 2106 IV B 1.
23. 149 F.3d 1368 (1998).

complex agglomeration of mutual funds, which State Street called its Hub and Spoke system. The CAFC compared this to a binary-coded decimal system, stating that whereas the patent in *Gottschalk* was denied because it did not have a useful purpose, this application indeed had a useful purpose, so the mutual fund system was patentable subject material:

> Today, we hold that the transformation of data, representing discrete dollar amounts, by a machine through a series of mathematical calculations into a final share price, constitutes a practical application of a mathematical algorithm, formula, or calculation, because it produces "a useful, concrete and tangible result"—a final share price momentarily fixed for recording and reporting purposes and even accepted and relied upon by regulatory authorities and in subsequent trades.

The ruling cites *Diamond* v. *Chakrabarty*, the case that allowed genes to be patented and that cited a congressional panel's commentary describing the scope of invention as "anything under the sun that is made by man."[24] In *State Street Bank* the court ruled that an algorithm used to conduct business fits that description.

But notice that the resulting "machine" was in no way an extension of the mathematical result: it simply applied a series of transformations to a few numbers, just as Flook's formula translated a few numerical measures into a number used to set off an alarm. Applying *State Street*'s reasoning—that an algorithm plus application is patentable—to *Parker* v. *Flook* would lead to exactly the opposite conclusion from that of the Supreme Court and would allow Flook's patent on an equation directly applied to a useful purpose to stand.

The only way to reconcile the rule that a pure equation is not patentable with the rule that the practical application of an equation is patentable is to ignore Gale and Shapley's comments on abstraction and impose an artificial division of labor: mathematicians would work with only pure numbers, and then other people would come along and apply those pure numbers to the real world. For example, mathematicians would only write equations like

24. *Diamond* v. *Chakrabarty*, 447 U.S. 303 (1980), cites Senate Report 1979, 82 Cong. 2 sess. (1952). Here is the original statement: "A person may have 'invented' a machine or a manufacture, which may include anything under the sun that is made by man, but it is not necessarily patentable under section 101 unless the conditions of the title are fulfilled."

$$P = Q \cdot exp(t \cdot i),$$

while financiers would take this equation and turn it into

(Payout) = (Quantity invested) $exp$(time · interest rate).

But to actual mathematicians, the two formulas are equivalent. As the saying goes, mathematics is invariant under changes of notation.[25] But law is not invariant under changes of notation. Under the *State Street* ruling, the first equation is a mere abstraction, whereas the second, a means of calculating compound interest on an investment, is patentable subject matter.

### Business Methods

As an aside, the *State Street* ruling also allowed business methods to be patented. The logic is very similar: there is no machine, no ephemeral manifestation of the idea to speak of, but the idea itself is the result of creativity, effort was expended in writing it down in sufficient detail, and the idea affects the physical world; therefore the business method should be patentable. The *State Street* ruling expresses its disdain for "the judicially-created, so-called 'business method' exception to statutory subject matter. We take this opportunity to lay this ill-conceived exception to rest."[26]

With the final coffin nail having been put in the presumption that an invention must demonstrate innovation in the manipulation of physical objects to be patentable, one may ask where the line should be drawn. If a patent is not based in substantial innovation in the physical realm, and if text in a programming language can be patented, then why not patent art or plain English? This reasoning is followed to its conclusion by Aharonian and Stim in *Patenting Art and Entertainment: New Strategies for Protecting Creative Ideas*, which offers abundant examples of utility patents for artistic designs, and in "A Potentially New IP: Storyline Patents," an article by Andrew F. Knight, the head of a Virginia firm in the business of helping authors apply for storyline patents.[27]

---

25. Attributed to University of Chicago math professor Paul Sally.
26. As with the rulings for software, this ruling did not ask whether patents on business methods would pass economic analysis. That is, does a monopoly on a method of providing goods or services expand the total efficiency of the market and the total amount and variety of goods and services available? But that is a question for another book.
27. Aharonian and Stim (2004); Knight (2004). Knight's article details how all the arguments that allowed software to be patentable subject matter apply to storylines as well.

## A Modern Example

As an example of how nonpatentable math becomes patentable, consider patent 6,735,568 (granted to Eharmony.com on May 11, 2004) for a "Method and system for identifying people who are likely to have a successful relationship." Despite a bit of window dressing about neural networks and verifying the results by running regressions on past matches, the gist of the process as claimed is this:

1. Ask candidates to fill out a survey.
2. Enter the data into a matrix.
3. Run a singular value decomposition (SVD) of the matrix to find the candidates' positions in an imaginary space.
4. Match candidates who are closest in the imaginary space.

Steps 1 and 2 are trivial, and given the positions calculated in step 3, step 4 is also easy (this is no traveling salesman problem!). All of the magic happens in step 3 (claim 11 of the patent). The mathematician readers will recognize the SVD (also known as principal component analysis, or factor analysis) as a standard method used in linear algebra to reduce data in many dimensions to fewer dimensions with a minimal loss of information (that is, a method for low-rank approximation). Social scientists will recognize it as a commonly used method of categorizing people; for example, political scientists use it to categorize members of Congress by their roll call votes, and anthropologists use it to determine whether people from different cultures perceive common stimuli such as colors differently.[28] Computer scientists are reminded that they just need to find the right library: for this the author suggests the GNU Scientific Library, whose `gsl_linalg_SV_decomp` function will do the entire SVD with one function call.

In short, Eharmony has taken a mathematical procedure from undergraduate linear algebra textbooks and applied it to a slightly novel setting by assigning names to the variables, calling $L_1$, for example, sexual passion and $L_2$ spirituality. The additional mathematical window dressing in the patent's other claims are also a set of standard procedures. Programmers must now beware: they are free to call the `gsl_linalg_SV_decomp` function only if they choose variable names sufficiently removed from Eharmony's.

---

28. On roll call votes, see Poole and Rosenthal (1985); on color recognition, Moore, Romney, and Hsia (2002).

### Jefferson's Opinion

As Jefferson made clear in the letter quoted earlier, he did not like the idea of patenting applications either: "I assume it is a Lemma, that it is the invention of the machine itself, which is to give a patent right, and not the application of it to any particular purpose, of which it is susceptible." He continues with some examples of how bad the system would be if this precept were not followed:

> If one person invents a knife convenient for pointing our pens, another cannot have a patent right for the same knife to point our pencils. A compass was invented for navigating the sea; another could not have a patent right for using it to survey land. A machine for threshing *wheat* has been invented in Scotland; a second person cannot get a patent right for the same machine to thresh *oats*, a third *rye*, a fourth *peas*, a fifth *clover*, &c. A string of buckets is invented and used for raising water, ore, &c., can a second have a patent right to the same machine for raising wheat, a third oats, a fourth rye, a fifth peas, &c?

A state machine is an informational tool that can be used for any computable task. As the law stands, a physical state machine applied to pencil design may have one patent, applied to pen design it may have another, applied to the problem of optimally threshing oats still another, and so on. According to Jefferson's logic, *Flook*, *State Street* and the Eharmony patents are for a mathematical process, which is a law of nature and is thus not patentable, which is applied to a novel application, which Jefferson believed should not be patentable either.

## The State of Patents Today

As just outlined, recent rulings have put the last nail in the coffin of legal arguments for restricting software patents on the basis of subject matter. *In re Alappat* dodged the question of whether software has physical manifestation, and *State Street* proclaimed that as long as there is some sort of useful application, the subject is not too abstract to be patented. Since the term *useful* is always interpreted in its broadest sense—anyone filing for a patent is probably going to find the claimed invention to be useful— one can expect almost *any* subject matter to be acceptable.

The USPTO has provided an abundance of evidence supporting my claim that it is impossible to distinguish between useful applications and abstract mathematical algorithms. For example, Eharmony renamed the variables in the singular value decomposition and patented the resulting application, but perhaps this was unnecessary: patent 6,807,536 is for "Methods and systems for computing singular value decompositions of matrices and low rank approximations of matrices"—no need to restrict such a useful mathematical process to any specific application.

Here is a sampling of other patented algorithms that mathematicians must have their lawyers check out before using. Inspection of the patents shows that the device or apparatus in some of the titles is a general-purpose computer with a program loaded. Each patent is for a certain method; your own method of calculating fast Fourier transforms (FFTs) may or may not be covered:

—5,835,392: Method for performing complex fast Fourier transforms
—5,886,908: Method of efficient gradient computation
—6,055,556: Apparatus and method for matrix multiplication
—6,078,938: Method and system for solving linear systems
—6,356,926: Device and method for calculating FFT
—6,434,582: Cosine algorithm for relatively small angles
—6,640,237: Method and system for generating a trigonometric function
—6,665,697: Fourier analysis method and apparatus calculating the Fourier factor $W_n$ utilizing trigonometric relations
—6,745,215: Computer apparatus, program, and method for determining the equivalence of two algebraic functions
—6,792,569: Root solver and associated method for solving finite field polynomial equations.

These are not anomalies or oversights by individual examiners. As Gale and Shapley explained, there is no difference between an application of an algorithm and the algorithm itself, and, as the Church-Turing thesis states, the algorithm and pure math are entirely equivalent. The courts tried to draw a line between these entirely equivalent classes, and the USPTO, dealing with real-world algorithms, was unable to hold that fictitious line. Thus the CAFC rulings mean that individuals or corporations can own a piece of mathematics.

## Drawing the Line between Hardware and Software

The courts' patentability line between applied and pure mathematical algorithms clearly failed to exclude mathematics from patentability.

Where, then, should the line be drawn to ensure that math is not patentable but machinery is?

The current state of law is that an equation *applied* to a real-world problem is patentable if the entire entity—general-purpose computer plus inventive algorithm—fits the requirements, but a better rule would be that an equation *extended* to a real-world problem is patentable. In other words, a machine would have to be built that may rely on mathematics but does something innovative beyond it. The design of such a machine would be patentable if its physical component(s) met the usual tests of novelty and nonobviousness. Being the extension of an equation, the machine would also be in line with the rule that it is not the idea behind a machine that should be patentable but the design of the machine itself. If the entire design consists of an equation, then there is nothing to be patented; if the design consists of an equation and a trivial machine, then there is still nothing to be patented; if the design is for a new and novel machine informed by mathematics, then there is every reason to grant a patent on the machine's design.

### State Machines and Their States

The extension rule makes it easy to bar pure mathematics from patentability, but does it ensure that inventions at the physical end of the spectrum remain patentable? Those who hope to profit from software patents claim that there is a slippery slope between hardware and software and no way to draw a bright line between the two. For example, Jonathan Schwartz, president and chief executive officer of Sun Microsystems, explains: "Viewed simplistically, computing hardware is software burned into and onto physical things. And over time, more and more routine software elements end up in hardware, for acceleration or optimization. SSL [Secure socket layer] accelerators, JVMs [Java virtual machines] on a chip, you name it. So, where do you draw the line on patents? Firmware? FPGA's [field-programmable gate arrays]? Silicon? Systems?"[29]

Despite its tone and obfuscatory acronyms, this question is easy to answer. Recall the discussion in chapter 3 distinguishing between physical state machines and the programs loaded onto them. By this distinction, an inventive physical implementation of a state machine (such as an

29. From Jonathan Schwartz's blog, October 18, 2004 (blogs.sun.com/roller/page/jonathan/20041018#interpreting_sun_s_kodak_settlement).

FPGA, a JVM on a chip, or a rubber-curing device) should be patentable, whereas the programs loaded onto them (firmware, a data structure) should not.

That is, the state per se is nothing but a mathematical equation, and applying it to a Turing machine is a *Flook*-like obvious extension of the equation. By contrast, an inventive physical state machine may be heavily informed by mathematics but would make a nontrivial extension of that mathematics into the physical world.

The physical Turing machine and the states the Turing machine takes are clearly distinct, and I suspect Jonathan Schwartz and even the CAFC would have little trouble distinguishing between the two in any given situation. The distinction between physical state machine and informational state comfortably achieves the goals of making machines patentable and math unpatentable, and of being easy to recognize.

### The FPGA

The FPGA lies dangerously close to the borderline between software and hardware. As such, it is an excellent case study for how the dichotomy between state machine and state can be used in practice to draw a line between the patentable and unpatentable.

When it ships from the factory, the FPGA is a grid of a few hundred thousand identical logic blocks. To oversimplify the details, one may think of every block as connected to all of its neighbors. Like a sculptor carving a block of marble, an engineer can erase most of the connections to leave a functioning logic circuit. The engineer programming the FPGA will first write an algorithm using a words-on-paper programming language and then run it through a compiler to produce a machine-code representation of a circuit diagram, which he then feeds into a machine that will blow out the appropriate connections to leave the desired circuit.

In other words, an FPGA lets a programmer turn his or her program directly into a physical device, bypassing the step of using a general-purpose state machine to interpret instructions. As such, it means that any program can be translated directly into an object that by most reasonable definitions is a novel device that should be patentable subject matter.

Indeed, by the *In re Alappat*-style physical device rule, this is wholly patentable. There is limited physical innovation in programming an FPGA—all of the physical processes have been patented by the manufacturers of the FPGA and its auxiliary tools. But physical innovation is not required so long as the whole—algorithm plus trivial physical extension—is novel. The program is also patentable by *State Street*'s subject matter rule, because the physical device that is the output to the story is a useful physical device.

Further, because the trivial final step of producing a physical state machine or a virtual device is an afterthought, the item is patentable in any manifestation. That is, under the current patent regime, the physical FPGA and its blueprint in program form are identical.

It is not just in their blogs that Sun's employees claim they cannot distinguish between a Java program and an FPGA; they also claim this in their patents. The patent for an "Apparatus for dynamic implementation of Java metadata interfaces" (6,918,122) boasts that this software can run on anything more advanced than a loaf of bread:

> In accordance with one embodiment of the present invention, the components, processes and/or data structures may be implemented using Java programs. . . . Different implementations may be used and may include other types of operating systems, computing platforms, computer programs, firmware, computer languages and/or general-purpose machines. In addition, those of ordinary skill in the art will readily recognize that devices of a less general purpose nature, such as hardwired devices, devices relying on FPGA (field programmable gate array) or ASIC (Application Specific Integrated Circuit) technology, or the like, may also be used without departing from the scope and spirit of the inventive concepts disclosed herein.

That is, it is the algorithm that matters, and therefore there is no need to concern oneself with the triviality of which physical manifestation the device will take. One could find comparable language in most—if not all—of the patents on computer-implemented algorithms.

By the rule that state machines may be patented but states may not, the FPGA would still be patentable, because it is a novel physical device. But this would not extend to other implementations of the algorithm, which do not produce a new state machine but simply execute on another state machine. That is, being able to encode a program onto an FPGA does not make the original program patentable—just the specific implementation as a physical FPGA. The state to which the FPGA has been set remains unpatented, so the scope of the patent does not cover all implementations of the algorithm in all languages on any general-purpose computing device.

Practically, it would be supremely difficult to design an FPGA using the same program and not infringe the physical device's patent. In other words, the program is effectively patented in the context of FPGAs. But if another engineer takes the algorithm burned onto the FPGA and implements it using a Java virtual machine on her PC, she has a wholly different machine. In fact, it is probably folly to do such a thing, because all of the optimizations inherent to the FPGA design are lost; the copycat engineer could probably have done better to write Java-specific code from scratch. That is, imitators who wish to use the detailed implementations that the designers worked to optimize would need to license the patent and thus reward the original designers for their efforts, while imitators who wish to use the broad algorithm are making use of the idea but not the detailed implementation, and since an idea cannot be patented, there is no need to call the lawyers and negotiate rights.

Broadly, an engineer may take two paths in implementing an algorithm. The first is the one that Sun took in patent 6,918,122: write a general algorithm that any state machine can execute. The second is the approach taken by a careful FPGA designer: write a program that is aimed at a single physical device.

In the first approach, there may be an innovative idea, but there is no innovative physical implementation, since applying a program to a stock state machine is a trivial application that anyone having ordinary skill in the art could do. The details of novel physical implementation are explicitly nil and therefore costless, while the patent is very broad and therefore blocks as many other designs as possible. By the rules of chapter 2, this is the worst case for a patent.

The second approach is indeed an innovative physical device and therefore does merit intellectual property protection, but only for a very specific implementation. In this form, a patent on a physical FPGA fits both of the rules from chapter 2: there are significant costs in designing the implementation and the costs of implementation are protected from those who would free-ride on the engineering behind the patent-holder's chip, but the patent does not arbitrarily exclude others from the use of alternate designs that the first designer had not conceived. Under the state/state machine rule, the patent-hungry are free to patent every algorithm imaginable as an FPGA, but because the patent covers only the specific implementation, the world's software programmers are still free to use the algorithm as they wish, and even creative FPGA designers will be able to design around the patent with sufficient ingenuity.

The process of designing an FPGA and the process of writing a program for a general-purpose computer may have much in common, but the steps the designers undertook is only one side of the patent balance; the other is the breadth of the resulting work.

As explained in chapter 2, it is essential that a patent have a balanced breadth. As explained in chapter 3, a claim on a program will, as a matter of mathematical fact, have a massive breadth, covering all implementations of that program in all languages, and even in pure mathematical forms. In practical terms of registers, relays, and resistors, there may be a fine line between a purpose-built machine and an algorithm on a general-purpose machine, but once the patent's coverage nudges over that fine line, its breadth explodes. Patent drafters have every interest in keeping that line hazy, but fortunately, a patent examiner is not burdened with determining which claims include only a reasonable range of innovative physical devices and which include all equivalent algorithms in all programming languages on all general-purpose state machines, because the examiner can restrict the wording of the claim to make sure the patent remains on the economically sensible side. The examiner may simply stipulate that a claim may not be construed to include implementation via a program on an uninnovative general-purpose state machine. The designer of an innovative physical design would be entirely unconcerned by such a clause, but it would effectively block the author of software who drafted a patent to imply that the design was a physically innovative device. Patents of reasonable breadth would continue to flourish, while those of the massive breadth of a software patent would be blocked.

## The Trouble with the Courts

However, the CAFC ruled that there would be no need to add restrictions on the breadth of a patent on software. Generally, the CAFC rulings here have rushed headlong into territory where past courts feared to tread. The ruling in *Flook* demanded no change without a congressional dictate: "We would require a clear and certain signal from Congress before approving the position of a litigant who . . . argues that the beachhead of privilege is wider, and the area of public use narrower, than the courts had previously thought."[30] Conversely, the CAFC did away with the concept

---

30. Here, Justice Stevens is quoting from the ruling in *Deepsouth Packing Co.* v. *Laitram Corp.* (406 U.S. 518, 531, 173 USPQ 769, 774).

of restrictions on software and business methods without the slightest signal from Congress. Whereas past courts such as the Supreme Court of 1853 have tried to strike a balance between public and private interests and ensure that patents do not become too broad, the CAFC has shown little or no objection to patents broad enough to cover pure math. While the Supreme Court's ruling in *Gottschalk* v. *Benson* barred a patent because it "would wholly pre-empt the mathematical formula and in practical effect would be a patent on the algorithm itself," the CAFC defined new rules that allowed patents on algorithms used to calculate fast Fourier transforms and cosines. This leads to the large academic literature on the CAFC, which asks two questions: is the CAFC more pro-patent than other courts, and given that the answer to the first question is so obviously yes, why?

As to why, there is abundant evidence that the CAFC is interested in expanding the scope of its jurisdiction. Also, whereas some courts are more willing to ask whether a certain patent regime is or is not good for the economy, the CAFC seems to be going out of its way to dodge such issues, focusing narrowly on whether the regime is or is not consistent with the broad wording of §101.

### The CAFC's Track Record

Before the CAFC was established in 1982, patent appeals were heard in various district courts. Up to then, the last year in which data were compiled on patent infringement cases was 1978, when slightly more than 40 percent of appellate trials found the patent in question valid and infringed. In 1982, after the CAFC was established, it found that the patent in question was valid and infringed in upward of 80 percent of infringement cases.[31] Since then, its rate of upholding patents has come down from this high, but on the whole the CAFC has shown itself to be much more pro-patent than the general district courts that came before it.

The key cases that established software patents (*Alappat, Lowry, State Street,* and even *AT&T* v. *Excel,* which I do not discuss here) overturned the rulings of the district courts.[32] Overall, the federal circuit affirmed at

31. Jaffe and Lerner (2004, p. 105).
32. Many are of the opinion that *Diamond* v. *Diehr* is the case that ushered software patents into law, but I am entirely unconvinced that the Court decided software should be patentable. Again, the ruling refers only to a rubber-curing machine and industrial equipment and does not address the question of general-purpose computers, whereas the four cases that the CAFC ruled upon directly do cover general-purpose computers.

least in part 86.3 percent of lower-court decisions and denied 17.1 percent at least in part. This suggests that these four cases, which vehemently denied the lower-court ruling, are rare—and they *are* rare, in the sense that they expanded the scope of the federal circuit's jurisdiction immensely.[33]

### Regulatory Capture

The federal district courts and the Supreme Court hear cases covering all of federal law; the CAFC hears mostly customs disputes and patent appeals and assigns a large proportion of the patent cases to a few judges.[34] This is an exceptional concentration of interest: the scope of patent law is decided by a few people who work on nothing but patents and who deal exclusively with patent lawyers. Of course, the natural candidates for such a judgeship are current patent lawyers.

The goal of a bureaucracy, according to most social scientists, is to maximize its budget.[35] For the USPTO, that means getting as many patent submissions as possible. For the courts, it means interpreting the law in a manner that puts as many fields of human endeavor under the court's scope as possible. After all, many judges are former patent lawyers and still have some interest in keeping the patent law business healthy. There is some evidence that the increase in the amount of patent litigation in recent years coincides with the pro-patent trend in the CAFC.[36] Furthermore, there is a 97 percent correlation between log(patent suits commenced) and log(number of active patent lawyers and agents).[37]

Swamped by the flood of software patents, the USPTO has been calling for more funding: the acting head of the agency, John W. Dudas, said that if funding is not forthcoming, the current two-year backlog among

33. Allison and Lemley (2000, p. 759); the statistics indicate that 3.4 percent of rulings were partly affirmed and partly denied. Some readers may wonder why the pre-CAFC district courts had generally been less pro-patent, while the CAFC affirmed most of the district court rulings. With the establishment of the new court, what were now the lower courts fell in line with the opinions of the CAFC and became increasingly pro-patent as well. However, the jurisdiction of the district court is much broader than that of the CAFC. Therefore changes in the scope of patent law have a proportionately smaller effect on the jurisdiction of the district courts.

34. Allison and Lemley (2000, esp. fn. 30).

35. Generally attributed to Niskanen (1971).

36. Landes and Posner (2003).

37. Landes and Posner (2003, p. 348).

all patents could quickly stretch to a five-year backlog.[38] This again indicates that the best party to make decisions about economically efficient patent laws is the legislative branch, whose jurisdiction and budget are not directly affected by the scope of patents. Much more evidence of regulatory capture has been provided by Adam Jaffe and Josh Lerner in their 2004 study on the U.S. patent system and the effects of the formation of the CAFC.[39]

### Worldview

In a less cynical vein, one could argue that working on patents all day might distort the worldview of even the most well-meaning judge. In the debate about establishing the CAFC, some feared that judges who worked on nothing but patents might put them at the center of the world.[40] Such judges would be inclined to allow more patents to stand than the general public would allow. The data support this story. Also, on broader questions of subject matter, specialized patent judges might believe that "everything invented by man under the sun" should be patentable. Indeed, CAFC rulings indicate that its judges are reluctant to invalidate patents based on the mathematical exception or a no-physical-manifestation heuristic.

In view of this overspecialization, the nonpartisan National Academy of Sciences recommends changing the method of selecting judges to bring some fresh economic thinking into patent rulings, arguing that the few appointments to the federal circuit intended to support the court's expertise in patent law "should not be confined to intellectual property practitioners and academics. Rather, the court's perspective should be broadened by appointing judges familiar with innovation more generally, including men and women with backgrounds in antitrust or finance law or, in addition to their legal training, in economics or economic history."[41]

38. John W. Schoen, "U.S. Patent Office Swamped by Backlog," *MSNBC News*, April 27, 2004 (www.msnbc.msn.com/id/4788834); FTC (2003).
39. Jaffe and Lerner (2004) mention regulatory capture by name on page 160, but the entire book is about how the courts and USPTO have been expanding their jurisdiction consistent with the regulatory capture hypothesis.
40. Landes and Posner (2003).
41. Merrill, Levin, and Meyers (2004, p. 87).

According to Arti Kaur Rai of the Duke University School of Law, the CAFC's pro-patent rulings reflect an underlying philosophy that patents should be treated like any other physical property:

> These statistical and doctrinal shifts, coupled with scattered commentary from particular Federal Circuit judges, suggests that at least some members of the Federal Circuit view patent rights as . . . comparable to rights in tangible property. While conventional economic analysis of patents is concerned with the deadweight loss and impediments to future innovation that patents may create . . . , an "ordinary property" view dismisses the possibility that patents create monopoly-like difficulties. Thus there is no reason to object to patents issuing for virtually all invention that is novel.[42]

This view is the source of endless frustration for economists and programmers. Economists write books and journal articles on the economic effects of patents, and programmers fill the Internet with commentary about how patents make their jobs harder, yet the courts ignore all of it. "Indeed, nothing in the court's [*State Street*] opinion even recognized the giant step it was taking in holding that all mathematical algorithms with any plausible 'usefulness' are patentable subject matter."[43]

As an economist who has written a book on the matter, I propose that we take the question out of the hands of the courts. The courts only interpret the laws passed by Congress. They do not ask the truly important policy question: do software patents do more economic good than harm? It is up to the Congress to ask this question directly, and to write a clear law of software patents based upon the answer.

In the words of the National Academy of Sciences: "The effects of this substantial de facto broadening of patent subject matter to cover information inventions are as yet unclear. Because this expansion has occurred without any oversight from the legislative branch and takes patent law into uncharted territories, it would be worthwhile to study this phenomenon to ensure that the patent expansion is promoting the progress of science and the useful arts, as Congress intended."[44] The following chapters will do exactly this.

42. Rai (2002, p. 67).
43. Rai (2002, p. 63).
44. National Academy of Sciences (2002), p. 195.

# CHAPTER FIVE

# Profiting from Overbroad Patents

What's wrong with the system of software patents that the courts have put in place? One set of problems stems from weaknesses in the patenting process that could be remedied by revised policies or more resources at the U.S. Patent and Trademark Office (USPTO), while other fundamental issues are rooted in the nature of software and software patents.

First, software patents are too broad, and unavoidably so. Since software patents typically apply to the broad description of an idea—the interface instead of the implementation—they can block competitors from developing and marketing hundreds of alternative implementations. Second, as explained in chapter 3, all software is a compound invention, so patents are much more likely to hold up innovation in software than in fields where inventors are less dependent on the work of others. These problems bedevil all industries to some degree, but software is always hit hardest. Moreover, the rapid pace of software development magnifies the negative impact.

## Do Software Patents Promote Innovation?

These problems are of particular concern because there is little evidence that software patents promote innovation—the usual justification for granting patents at all. Few scholars have addressed this question, primarily because of the difficulty of coming up with an appropriate measure of innovation. Most studies of how external economic factors affect innovation use a count of patents as the proxy for innovativeness, but some other measure is clearly required in this case.[1]

Using investment in research and development as a proxy for innovation, James Bessen of Research on Innovation and Robert M. Hunt of the Federal Reserve Bank of Philadelphia found that companies heavy in software patents do *less* research than expected.[2] A lively debate followed the release of these results, with two scholars at the American Enterprise Institute–Brookings Joint Center for Regulatory Studies, Robert Hahn and Scott Wallsten, arguing that the numbers actually showed the expected positive correlation.[3] Bessen and Hunt have posted a rebuttal to the rebuttal online.[4]

But even if Hahn and Wallsten are correct, and patents do shift research funds toward those fields of applied mathematics that are patentable, such gains need to be weighed against the means by which patents can also *stifle* technological progress. A small gain in the rate of innovation, visible if one looks at the data one way but not another, may not be enough to offset the negative effects patents have on the implementation of new software.

## Trouble at the USPTO

Software is the canary in the USPTO's coal mine. Although problems with the overall system have touched every industry, they plague software more than other fields because of its unique aspects.

### Novelty

Because claims are innocent until proven guilty and so many inventions are obvious to people who have already seen the patent, patent examiners are encouraged not to use their ex post intuition about whether a patent is obvious. Instead, they are expected to go through a patent claim by claim to find proof that each should be invalidated or

---

1. Trajtenberg (1990).
2. Bessen and Hunt (2004a).
3. Hahn and Wallsten (2003). This paper was partly funded by Microsoft.
4. Bessen and Hunt (2004b).

restricted. Being inundated by applications, however, USPTO examiners must forgo a full search to invalidate all claims and must let them pass with minimal examination. Examiners have between fifteen and thirty hours to process a patent, which may contain up to hundreds of claims; those claims for which specific existing literature (*prior art*) cannot be located in that time frame must be left to stand as given.[5]

The *Manual of Patent Examining Procedure* (*MPEP*) includes a single paragraph on the subject of searching prior art for computer-related literature.[6] Here is the key sentence: "Generally, a thorough search involves reviewing both U.S. and foreign patents and non-patent literature."[7] In practice, this often becomes a search heavily biased toward U.S. patents.

As an aid to the search, the applicant is obligated to list all relevant prior publications or patents in the application. According to one industry observer, 58 percent of software patents granted in 2003 referred *only* to prior patents and made no mention of prior art in existing software or in computer science journals.[8] This would not be a problem in most other fields, where patent records go back either to the birth of the field or the birth of the United States, but since most software patents were applied for after the 1998 *State Street* ruling, the prior art embodied in existing patents is not entirely in line with the prior art pertaining to what computer scientists are doing.[9] It is still much easier to invent a process of computing that has not been patented than to invent a process of computing that has not been used by practitioners.

As Adam Jaffe and Josh Lerner explain, the USPTO's system gives examiners an incentive to approve easily:

> Patents examiners are given one point when they complete an initial review of a patent and another point when the application is ultimately allowed or rejected. . . . But applicants can modify and appeal patents that are initially rejected, thereby postponing the earning of the second productivity point. Thus, a rejected patent will typically consume much more of an examiner's time than one

5. Merrill, Levin, and Meyers (2004).
6. USPTO (2001).
7. *MPEP* §2106, section III (p. 2106–10).
8. Estimate from Greg Aharonian, editor of the Internet Patent News Service, personal communication, July 22, 2004. He indicates that prior years had been worse: 1980, 91 percent; 1985, 80 percent; 1990, 73 percent; 1995, 64 percent; 2000, 65 percent.
9. Ibid.

that is allowed after the initial application. This scheme creates an obvious incentive for examiners to "go easy" on applicants and allow their patents to be granted.[10]

Because patents must pass unless proven not novel and examiners do not have the time to find proof, the tendency in the review process is to let patents slide through for all types of invention. This is bad policy. On the margin, between the almost obvious cases in which patents should be granted and the actually obvious ones in which they should not, an examiner could make two types of errors, whose costs need to be balanced:

—Type I: A patent is granted when it should have been denied. The applicant probably got the patent so that it could be enforced, in which case what is effectively a monopoly is granted where it should not have been, and the market becomes less efficient. If the patent goes to litigation, the parties will likely spend between thousands and millions of dollars on overturning the erroneous granting.

—Type II: A patent is denied when it should have been granted. Some inventors will respond to the news by redoubling their efforts on new patents, to make sure that their future applications are several steps beyond the borderline for obvious ideas. Those unable to pass this borderline would be discouraged from continuing to claim nearly obvious ideas as their own and might instead take up accounting. Whether this would be a loss or not is debatable.

In short, the cost of a Type II error for a borderline-obvious patent may be very low, whereas the cost of a Type I error may be astronomical. So why does the USPTO bias its system to favor Type I errors over Type II errors, for physical inventions as well as software?

### The Review Process

All this would not be a problem if the review process made it easy to discern what examiners had missed during post-patent review. But the USPTO rarely permits a second review, and the only alternative is the court system, which can cost millions of dollars. Recommendation 1 in the Federal Trade Commission's (FTC's) report on improving the patent system is to implement a new post-patent review process.[11]

---

10. Jaffe and Lerner (2004, p. 136).
11. FTC (2003).

Under the existing regime, requests for reexamination face heavy restrictions. A plaintiff may file a request with the USPTO only to question novelty or nonobviousness and after filing may provide no further input or commentary on the USPTO's process or decisions. Until November 2002, the plaintiff could not even dispute the findings in federal court.[12]

There is no way to dispute a patent on the grounds of inappropriate breadth or subject matter.[13] For example, one cannot argue, in the words of the *Gottschalk* v. *Benson* ruling, that the mathematical patents on page 63 "would wholly pre-empt the mathematical formula and in practical effect would be a patent on the algorithm itself." Reversing these patents would require either a huge amount of litigation or an act of Congress to change the rules of reexamination.

These heavy restrictions make it difficult for a company to harass a patent-holder via the USPTO—or to have truly bad patents reversed. Even the review process leans heavily toward Type I errors. After the plaintiff provides the limited information prescribed, the reexamination proceeds along approximately the same lines as the initial review; in some cases, the same examiner who granted the patent performs the reexamination.[14] The chance of repeating the same mistakes is thus higher than it needs to be.

Without an easy way for the USPTO to reverse its errors, the only alternative is to rely on the court system, which is the most expensive and inefficient means of overturning a patent that one could imagine. According to one FTC panelist, it can cost $5 million to $7 million to litigate a biotechnology patent case.[15] Douglas Brotz, principal scientist at Adobe Systems, expressed his and Adobe's frustration with patents and their associated legal expenses at a public hearing in January 1994:

> The emergence in recent years of patents on software has hurt Adobe and the industry. A "patent litigation tax" is one impediment to our financial health that our industry can ill-afford. . . . Revenues are being sunk into legal costs instead of into research

12. Plaintiffs may request an *inter partes* review, in which the plaintiff is more involved in the process, but from 1999 to 2003 the USPTO granted only four such requests. FTC (2003, sec. 5, p. 16).
13. FTC (2003).
14. Jaffe and Lerner (2004, pp. 153–54).
15. FTC (2003, chap. 3, p. 22).

and development. It is clear to me that the Constitutional mandate to promote progress in the useful arts is not served by the issuance of patents on software.

Let me illustrate this burden with some figures. The case *Information International Incorporated* v. *Adobe, et al.,* was filed five years ago. Last year the trial court ruled for Adobe, finding no infringement. In December the Appeals Court for the Federal Circuit unanimously affirmed that judgment. Yet, in that time, it has cost Adobe over four and a half million dollars in legal fees and expenses. I myself have spent over three thousand five hundred hours of my time—that's equivalent to almost two years of working time—and at least another thousand hours was spent by others at Adobe. The Chairman of the Board spent a month at the trial. This type of company behavior would not be high on anyone's list of ways to promote progress.[16]

### Breadth

A patent on an interface is, almost by definition, a much broader patent than a comparable patent on an implementation. Notice that most of the software patents and applications discussed to this point, such as those in figures 2-4 and 3-2 (the tabbed browsing and the XML-reading patents), are for a flowchart, which describes only what the functions will do—they cover the interface but not the implementation. As discussed in the section on gaming on page 80, these patents apply to all implementations and block all competitors from entering a broad market.

To give another example, here is the abstract for patent 5,132,992 (to Yurt and Browne, July 1992), for an "Audio and video transmission and receiving system" that covers every sound or moving picture on the Internet: "A system of distributing video and/or audio information employs digital signal processing to achieve high rates of data compression. The compressed and encoded audio and/or video information is sent over standard telephone, cable or satellite broadcast channels to a receiver specified by a subscriber of the service, preferably in less than real time, for later playback and optional recording on standard audio and/or video tape."

---

16. Public Hearing on Use of the Patent System to Protect Software Related Inventions: Transcript of Proceedings, Wednesday, January 26, 1994, San Jose Convention Center (http://lpf.ai.mit.edu/Patents/testimony/statements/adobe.testimony.html).

The patent fails to give the details of "digital signal processing," the method of compression, the method of encoding, or the method of playback. To summarize the fifty-eight claims of the patent: the sender takes a video or audio clip, cuts it into packets, compresses them, and sends them down the wire to a receiver, which decompresses the packets and plays them. The patent is even agnostic about the type of wire. It does not mention the Internet, so TV cable or anything else that uses a digital signal is covered by this patent as well. Because it is so general, practitioners would have trouble finding this patent. It never uses the word "Internet," the term "streaming media" had not yet been coined, and it fails to mention any of the protocols that are commonly used on the Internet today.

The modular implementation/interface structure of computer science is wonderful because any black box in a program can be replaced with any of a dozen black boxes with a similar interface. The transmission and receiving system could just as easily use the MPEG 1 or MPEG 4 format, the RealMedia format, the QuickTime format, the AVI format, or a dozen others—so the patent covers all of these. Again, if the USPTO had granted a patent on only a single implementation, the hassles engendered by such breadth would not have arisen. Nonetheless, it is content to grant patents on interfaces.

### Search

Software's patent problems are compounded by the tribulations of search. Summing these up for an FTC panel, patent lawyer R. Lewis Gable observed that it is impossible to reliably search existing software patents:

> You're trying to advise a client who's coming in and saying "Can I enter this field and are there third-party patents out there that I will infringe?" . . . There's no way to find out whether your client will just be walking into an infringement problem. And the thing that often happens, and it's sort of tragic for the individual small investor: they put a lot of money and a lot of effort into this process and two or three years down the line . . . they found out another patent has issued that covers their invention and they're barred from using it.[17]

17. FTC (2002, pp. 118–19).

Software patents are uniquely difficult to search because there are so many levels at which a program can violate a patent: the line, the function, the library, the program that ties the library's elements together—any of these could be infringing. Some patents cover single functions, such as the pop-up window of figure 1-1. Others are for components of larger programs, such as the functions that enable browsing with the <tab> key. Still others have broad coverage: the streaming media patent, for example, has a wealth of applications, thanks to the abstract nature of mathematics-in-code.

Imagine designing a machine, say, an oat thresher, and having to do a patent search—first on the overall concept just implemented, then on every method of connecting two parts, then on every bolt in the machine—only to find that the machine is a special case of a pure mathematical algorithm that makes no reference to oats, threshing, or bolts. In view of the modular structure of software and the fact that new methods are continuously devised on every level, the search problem is orders of magnitude more complex in software than in traditional fields. As a result, many just save themselves the trouble and assume that they are infringing something.

## Gaming with Broad Patents

The process allows too many undeserving patents to get easy approval and makes overturning them supremely difficult. The subject matter along with the court rulings (see chapter 4) have made software patents especially broad and far-reaching. Nobody knows for certain if every function in a program is patent-free. This sets the stage for a wide array of dirty tricks by any business armed with a patent arsenal. Such abuses can befall any patentable endeavor, but software is usually hit hardest because of the breadth of its patents, the building-block structure of software programs, and the great uncertainty as to what a given software patent covers and what patents cover a given product.

### Blocking Patents and Compound Inventions

A *blocking patent* is one that applies or improves another.[18] For example, Emily Rose may invent a skin patch that administers Prozac in a steady,

---

18. This type of patent is often more optimistically referred to as an "improving patent." Some reserve the name "blocking patent" for those patents that are applied for

perpetual stream. Eli Lilly cannot administer Prozac in this way unless it licenses Emily's patch, but Emily's patch is useless unless she licenses Prozac from Eli Lilly. They are mutually blocked and have a strong incentive to work together to create a common product and share the profits.

Eli Lilly is reasonably likely to allow a cross-licensing agreement. More generally, whenever someone needs an invention as an ingredient in a more complex recipe, there is a good chance that they will be able to get access to the invention for a modest licensing fee. The arts and sciences make progress, and the original inventor makes a living.

Allocating rights to the components of an invention via blocking patents is sensible for goods relying on a small number of inventions, but as discussed in chapter 3, all software stands on the shoulders of dozens of libraries that came before it. If Emily Rose wants to write an electronic address book and needs to contact one company for permission to use its sorting algorithm, and another company for permission to describe people using a certain data structure, still another for permission to implement navigation with the <tab> key, and so on, she will spend so much more time with lawyers than with coders that she may just give up the project. As Ronald Mann's University of Texas study points out, actual producers faced with this situation typically do not throw up their hands but instead write the software and resign themselves to the fact that if it sells well they will eventually hear from the appropriate patent lawyers.

This is in line with Coase's theorem, which can loosely be taken to say that the allocation of property rights does not matter for achieving (Pareto) optimality, but that transaction costs do. Therefore property rights should be allocated so as to minimize transaction costs.[19] By this logic, giving dozens of individuals the rights needed to implement a single program would be suboptimal.

### Complex Industries

Wesley Cohen, Richard Nelson, and John Walsh (of Carnegie Mellon, Columbia University, and the University of Illinois at Chicago, respectively) interviewed employees working for a wide range of firms in which patents

---

solely to make life difficult for competitors, but improvement-type patents are much more common.

19. Coase (1960). Although Coase's 1960 paper is primarily about the equivalence of different allocations in a frictionless market, the bulk of his research was about the means and costs of bargaining—the transaction costs.

are relevant.[20] They distinguished between industries with simple products consisting of only one or a few patentable components and industries with complex products involving hundreds of patents. Complex products include computers, electrical equipment, electronic components, and instruments. Since all software is built on an infinite tower of prior software, it is the perfect example of a complex industry. Cohen and his colleagues found both anecdotally and statistically that firms in complex industries are more likely to patent for the purpose of cross-licensing:

> Because no one firm can move ahead on developing and commercializing new technology without access to rival technology, incumbents can use their patents as bargaining chips either to compel their inclusion in cross-licensing or at least secure the freedom to move ahead on similar technological efforts without being sued. We call this use of patents "block to play" because by compelling either access to rival technology or at least protecting against suits by incumbents, it facilitates a firm's participation in a broad domain of technological activity.[21]

One executive of a firm manufacturing communications equipment stated: "Mostly, your patents are used in horse trading. You come together and say, 'Here's our portfolio.' In our industry, things all build on each other. We all overlap on each other's patents. Eventually we come to some agreement: 'You can use ours and we can use yours.'"[22]

This sort of dealing is *rent seeking*: the process of allocating the spoils of productive work already completed. Rent seeking is inevitable and often a small part of a larger productive activity. On the other hand, a system used only for rent seeking to the point of crowding out productive activity is destructive. If Company A could extract $2 million from Company B by burning a million dollars' worth of goods, it would do so without hesitation, but the society as a whole is a million dollars poorer.

When Cohen and his colleagues asked manufacturers directly why they patent their processes, they found the computer industry more interested in rent-seeking uses than productive uses. Table 5-1 presents the responses for all industries, with special attention to the computer industry (which includes both hardware and software), semiconductors, and

20. Cohen, Nelson, and Walsh (2000).
21. Cohen, Nelson, and Walsh (2000, p. 22).
22. Cohen, Nelson, and Walsh (2000, p. 19).

**Table 5-1. Motives for Patenting: The Computer Industry versus Other Industries**
Percent of respondents

| Why patent? | Computers | Semiconductors | Electronic components | All industries | Percent difference computers vs. all industries |
|---|---|---|---|---|---|
| Prevent suits | 88.2 | 58.3 | 41.7 | 46.5 | +41.7 |
| For use in negotiations | 70.6 | 50.0 | 41.7 | 37.0 | +33.6 |
| Prevent copying | 70.6 | 91.7 | 88.3 | 77.6 | −7.0 |
| Blocking | 58.8 | 58.3 | 58.3 | 63.6 | −4.8 |
| Licensing revenue | 35.3 | 41.7 | 25.0 | 23.3 | +12.04 |
| Enhance reputation | 23.5 | 25.0 | 33.3 | 34.0 | −10.5 |
| Measure performance | 0.0 | 0.0 | 0.0 | 5.0 | −5.0 |

related electronic components.[23] In other industries, the most common use of patents is to protect an innovation from being copied as per their intended purpose discussed in chapter 2. But in the computer industry, the most common reason for patenting is to gain a defense against lawsuits; protecting the innovation comes second, along with use in rent-seeking negotiations. Furthermore, the difference in responses between the computer industry and the overall industries surveyed indicate that its rent-seeking motivations are more common in relation to the norm.

This is not to say that defense and rent seeking are as prevalent in all complex industries. The survey results from the semiconductor and the electronic component industries (which build the parts for physical state machines) match the general pattern: their most likely motive by far is to maintain a distinct product, and blocking and defense are distant runners-up in both industries.

### Patent Thickets

For the most part, the horse trading that goes on among those who already hold enough patents is an unproductive waste of time, but with one significant side effect: it locks new entrants out of the market. Larger firms have *patent thickets* of hundreds or even thousands of related patents. Firms with dense thickets frequently exchange the rights to other

23. Cohen, Nelson, and Walsh (2000). The survey elicited 17 responses from firms in the computer industry, 12 in semiconductors, 12 in electronics, and a total of 674. Another survey, on product patents, showed similar results.

thickets. Here is Bill Gates, chief executive officer of Microsoft, describing the patent relationship between Microsoft and its competitors:

> It was probably 14 years or so ago when IBM, as part of their relationship with us, came and visited me and said they'd be willing to license their patents to us. And we said, oh, patents, wow, you want to license your patents to us. In fact, we did enter into an agreement with IBM, which IBM has done with many others, Microsoft has done with many others, where we had a certain type of cross-license. And I'd say year after year, certainly subsequent to that, it's something we've put a lot of energy into. . . . Just in the last year, examples of this are our cross-license with SAP; an IP [intellectual property] license with Sun as part of our new relationship with them. . . . So a lot of activity, a lot of visibility.[24]

What about those outside the club of large thicket-holders, whose one or two patents will never match IBM's thousands of patents? Can they produce software and also make money from cross-licensing? Legal scholar Ronald Mann interviewed developers and found that small firms do actually survive in the patent thicket—but only by treading lightly. One developer at a small software company who was asked about the possibility of suing IBM over a patent held by his firm told Mann: "IBM probably could sue us on 20 patents if they looked hard at what we do. But we don't want to have that relationship with them. Legal fees aside, we could lose everything."[25] Although these patent thickets clearly exist, it seems that IBM, for one, has so far failed to drop its sword of Damocles on the heads of start-ups. Yet as firms grow larger, Mann observes, this potential typically becomes a reality, and then having patents as bargaining chips becomes important: "Nevertheless, a patent to offset IBM's potential claim is of little value until the day when IBM demands royalties. IBM typically does not ask for royalties until the firm is earning sufficient revenues to justify the inquiry."[26]

Gary L. Reback, a Silicon Valley attorney, tells the story of how the company spun off from the Stanford University network (Sun) appeared on IBM's radar:

24. Financial analyst meeting, July 29, 2004 (www.microsoft.com/msft/speech/FY04/GatesFAM2004.mspx).

25. Mann (2004, p. 35).

26. Mann (2004, p. 44).

A team of IBM patent lawyers went to Sun Microsystems Inc. in the 1980s and claimed that the then start-up was infringing on seven of its patents. After Sun engineers explained why they were not infringing, the IBM lawyers responded that with 10,000 patents, they would be sure to find some infringement somewhere. . . . IBM said Sun could "make this easy and pay us $20 million." After some negotiation on the amount, Sun cut a check.[27]

These stories entirely corroborate the fact that IBM owns a patent thicket, and that it uses that patent thicket to gain revenue. Indeed, the 22,357 patents granted to IBM between 1993 and 2002 have earned it $10 billion in licensing fees.[28]

The extreme characterization would be that IBM sues all competitors out of existence, or that people cannot navigate the endless maze of paperwork needed to secure a dozen or a hundred patents before sitting down and writing code, but such a characterization is a myth. People will write the software they intended to write, and IBM, being a reasonable company, will allow them to do so. It is in IBM's best interest to have a wide range of software providers who all work on expanding the software market in productive and profitable ways—and who all pay IBM a percentage while doing so.

So patents are commonly used as bargaining chips between firms that want to hammer out license exchange agreements, and depending on the patents held, money changes hands from the small firm to IBM, or perhaps between IBM and Microsoft. Incumbents can guarantee that they will profit from future innovations by trading and enforcing their existing stable of patents. But there is little if any evidence that this expensive licensing game has anything to do with the process of new innovation or producing valuable software.

### The Hold-Up Problem

Even a large firm that holds most of the relevant patents in an industry may still have infringement problems. If one subroutine out of 10,000 lines of code involves a patented work, then the entire program is infringing. If the firm is notified of this before it distributes the program, it can simply replace the existing subroutine with an unpatented one. But the

27. As told by Krim (2003).
28. Krim (2003). An indeterminate number of these are hardware patents.

patent may be so broad that whatever the firm does would still tread on the patent. In such a case, where the entire program is held up by a small subelement, the person with the patent on that subelement can prevent the program from being used until quite large royalties are paid.

Better still, the patent-holder can wait until the program is on the market, and profits have been counted. Then the holder can sue for damages up to or above the full profits from the product—recall that Kodak extracted $92 million from Sun over patent infringement in *free* software. Although Sun's years of development of a new language that runs on dozens of platforms clearly dwarfed the work behind Kodak's patents on tables mapping object types to applications, there is no rule that damages should be proportional to the importance of the patent, however one would measure such a thing. Infringement either exists or does not.

Another notable example of the problem arises in *Eolas v. Microsoft*. Eolas is a company with no products of any sort, but it has a small patent portfolio. It claimed that it had a patent over a certain facet of Internet Explorer (IE) code that made use of the HTML-standard embed and object tags. Since IE had been distributed by Microsoft for years before the complaint was brought, the courts granted Eolas $521 million in ex post damages.[29] Like Java, IE has lived most of its life as free software.

The embed and object tags are only two of dozens of tags in the HTML standard. For example, the frame tag is notoriously difficult to use without violating Southwestern Bell Corporation's patents 5,933,841 and 6,442,574—and then there are the menus, the toolbars, the registry database, and tens of thousands of lines of supporting code gluing it all together. The $521 million Microsoft owes to Eolas did nothing to protect Microsoft from litigation over any other potential patents.

To summarize the game so far, one can basically assume (as Ronald Mann's interviewees did) that *all* software infringes on an IBM patent. A software author's main concern is to minimize the probability that IBM will pursue action, and if it does, to minimize the licensing fees. Holding one's own patents lowers the likelihood, as does staying small and under the radar. If a company's patent holdings grow in proportion to revenues, it will likely stay on level ground with IBM—but then none of this is nec-

---

29. Microsoft eventually influenced the USPTO to invalidate Eolas's patent, but Eolas has found ways to keep the lawsuit afloat. For the intricacies of the suit to date, see Crouch (2004).

essarily protection from firms like Eolas, which have no products and therefore no interest in cross-licensing.

Edward J. Black, president and CEO of the Computer and Communications Industry Association, summarized the situation in testimony to the FTC: "In too many different places [software patenting] has lost its fundamental engine, which is that it's supposed to be the dynamo and the legal structure that really promotes innovation. . . . [T]hat's not its core function[;] . . . the core function is business strategy, gaming, squeezing players out, preventing people from wanting to take risks."[30]

### Submarine Patents

Inventors are sometimes ahead of their time, and when other researchers catch up, they are surprised to see that their brilliant new ideas are actually old news, and even patented. Although this happens in every industry, it is more of a problem for the software industry because the product cycles are short, the database of software patents is impossible to search, and software lives and dies on its interoperability with other software. Mark Webbink, senior vice president and general counsel of Red Hat, Inc., explains: "It may be years beyond the time that a particular piece of technology has hit the marketplace before it is evident that it, in fact, is covered by a form of patent protection."[31]

Since searching the patent literature to determine whether an idea is someone's property is so difficult, the optimal strategy for many inventors is to hide their work in plain sight, losing it in the sea of patents. If they are lucky, one of their ideas will be patented and become an industry standard (via a contract, imitation, or independent derivation), and then they can wait for the standard to take off. This requires patience, but there is enough time. Since the computer industry changes so rapidly, a software interface can rise from obscurity to a universal standard well within the twenty-year life of a patent. When enough software is built around the standard, the patent-holder can surface. Vendors will acquiesce to paying licensing fees rather than suddenly find their product incompatible with every other piece of software.[32]

---

30. FTC (2002, p. 138).
31. FTC (2002, pp. 99–100).
32. The term "submarine patent" is usually used more restrictively to refer to patents that are deliberately held up in USPTO review. While under review, an invention is kept secret, so that if the patent application is rejected the applicant may still protect the invention as a trade secret. But others who are ignorant of the patent's progress may have implemented it by the

This strategy twists the social contract, relying on ignorance and over-sight rather than producing a product of higher quality. Instead of adver-tising an innovation and providing clear and fair licensing terms, a sub-marine patent-holder keeps potential buyers in the dark until they make decisions that they will regret after learning the patent-holder's terms. Examples of such innovations abound, including GIFs (files in the Graph-ics Interchange Format), MP3s, and streaming media.

*GIFs.* Most of the small drawings on the typical web page, such as arrows, logos, and cartoons, are in the Graphics Interchange Format. Part of the format's appeal is that it includes a compression scheme, the LZW algorithm (by Abraham Lempel, Jacob Ziv, and Terry Welch), which allows the picture to be sent down the wire quickly. Welch described the mathematical algorithm in a journal article—and in June 1983, just before it was published, he also applied for a patent on the scheme, with the company now known as Unisys as the assignee.[33] Meanwhile, the designers of the GIF standard used the LZW algorithm in a form they had seen in a peer-reviewed journal and made their results public. GIF took off and is now a well-supported standard.

Unisys, the owner of patent 4,558,302, subsequently sent letters assert-ing its ownership to everyone who writes software that can save images in GIF. Most just paid the GIF tax Unisys demanded (0.45 percent of unit sale price, minimum 10¢ per unit, maximum $10 per unit).[34] Authors of free software paid a different price: they had to cripple their software so as not to handle GIFs.[35]

*MP3s.* The International Standards Organization formed a committee, the Motion Picture Experts Group, to design a standard for the trans-mission of media by digital means. The first phase of the project focused on media that move data at a relatively slow speed, with layer III of that phase concentrating on audio. The reader is probably familiar with the

---

time the application emerges from the USPTO. Because of this, patent applications are now published 18 months after they arrive at the USPTO. Software patents are difficult to search even when published, so a patent is still effectively hidden even after it enters the public record. Hence in the context of software it is reasonable to expand the term to any invention that practitioners do not know about until informed via a royalty demand.

33. Welch (1984).

34. Amusingly enough, IBM has a patent on LZW encoding as well (patent 4,814,746); even USPTO patent examiners have trouble determining whether a software algorithm is already patented. See Battilana (2004).

35. Unisys's patent expired on June 20, 2003, and so programs involving it have since been uncrippled.

ISO MPEG-1 layer III standard by its colloquial name: MP3. Data had to move over a relatively narrow bandwidth, and it so happened that the Fraunhofer Institute for Integrated Circuits, a German research contractor, had done extensive prior work designing a standard for compressing audio data—and had patented the results (U.S. patents 5,579,430 and 5,742,735, among many others). After the MP3 format flourished and became an accepted standard that almost all audio software supports, the Fraunhofer Institute wrote to as many makers of MP3-creating and playing software and hardware as it could find to point out that its work is patented.

This is the perfect example of the submarine patent. Most people assumed that a standard may be freely used, and the fact that nobody thought it would cost anything certainly accounts in part for the popularity of MP3. Fraunhofer made no effort to dispel this belief until it started sending out royalty demands.

The damage has now been done, however, and people are much more wary of standards. Even when a standards body claims that its standards are patent-free, it simply cannot guarantee that it is not treading on any of the 170,000 existing software patents, or any of the pending applications at the USPTO that will be made public after the standard is published.

**Streaming Media.** Acacia Technologies is in the business of bringing submarine patents to the surface: it buys patents that match implementations by practitioners and then sues the practitioners. As of this writing, its prized possession is patent 5,132,992, the vaguely worded "Audio and video transmission and receiving system" from page 78.[36] According to an Acacia press release from June 15, 2004, Acacia is suing nine cable and satellite companies; anyone receiving digital cable might be a contributory infringer of this patent.

This is a case where everything discussed in this book went wrong. To begin with, as applied to most media, like the Internet, this patent is obvious. Since all data on the Internet are in packets, and since audio is compressed using a format such as MP3 (and video is compressed using another part of the MPEG-1 standard), the patent's new contribution to Internet media is that one side sends a media clip and the other side receives it.

There was nothing like this in the patent literature in 1992 because it had just never occurred to anybody to file a patent on this sort of thing

36. A lengthy discussion of Acacia's history and methods can be found in Cherry (2004).

before. However, the lack of prior patent art does not mean that a practitioner could not have come up with the process patented. The fact that nine cable and satellite companies and countless streaming media companies online all implemented this patent without knowing of its existence is a strong indication of its obviousness as written.

## The Instability of Existing Patents

Being so obvious and so broad, the streaming media patent may well be overturned eventually. In the meantime, nine companies are forced to occupy their legal teams in defending against the patent in court. Perhaps the patent will be reexamined by the USPTO and invalidated before the trials end; perhaps the defendants will have to pay Acacia. Because the patent is highly questionable, the defendants and the media industry at large are unsure of the outcome, and the world becomes a more uncertain place.

The economically optimal lawsuit is one that never happens. At best, the engineers know the rules of what they may or may not use; without involving lawyers, the education is cheap. If company B needs to use company A's patented technology, then B arranges clear licensing terms with A to use its technology, which is modestly expensive. Failing this, company A writes a cease-and-desist letter to company B, threatening to sue if company B continues to use its patented technology. Company B consults with its lawyers, who determine that the chance of having the patent struck down is minuscule, so the lawsuit would be a waste of effort, and the two companies arrive at some sort of settlement without going to trial; this is more expensive. Failing this, companies A and B go to trial, spending millions on legal fees.

How far companies A and B move along this chain of wasted expense depends heavily on the clarity of patent law and the patents themselves. The best laws are understood by all, the next best require occasional clarification in specific situations, and the worst are never clarified unless parties engage in full-blown litigation.

The software field is filled with patents that *could* be struck down. To make matters worse, the law is extremely complex: In contrast to the single paragraph on searching prior art, the MPEP includes eight pages of hairsplitting case law that attempts to establish what a patentable computer-related invention is.[37] The threat inherent in the cease-and-

37. MPEP 2100-10–2100-18.

desist letter ("We will take you to court and we will certainly win") is simply not credible.[38]

The social benefit from granting patents lies not in handing monopolies to those who have done good work in the past, but in motivating the researchers of today to continue to invent new technologies. If every conceivable technology is already patented, the patent system is directly frustrating its own goal. Submarine patents such as those mentioned earlier and the long list of related lawsuits in chapter 1 all serve as deterrents to new inventors, warning them that the software industry is a well-seeded minefield that they had best stay out of. In every industry, inventors are aware that they must be careful to search existing patents before embarking on any major projects, but chemists and engineers are not in the habit of assuming that *anything* they invent will infringe on some unknown party's patents. The patent mines in the physical fields are much less dense and much more clearly marked than in the software field.

If all software patents were fully valid and enforceable, and all programmers knew that they had to have a license from IBM, Novell, and Microsoft before sitting down to write any code, the world might still be better off than it is at present. Programmers would not inadvertently break the law, meaning that no lawsuits would be filed. They would not write code thinking that it was their own work only to later discover that they were implementing somebody else's patent. In equilibrium, few people would write code, but those who did would know exactly where they stood and would expend resources producing good products instead of playing legal games.

But this is as remote from the current state of affairs as can be. As chapter 6 makes clear, today's software market is crowded with a massively decentralized network of programmers, all of whom make some contribution to the world's code base but feel the constant threat of patent litigation at their backs.

---

38. This does not mean that company B will certainly go to trial, since the cost may not be worth the effort. Because the benefits to striking down a bad patent are distributed among many users whereas the cost is borne entirely by the company that tries to strike it down, there is a collective action problem in defeating bad patents, so the patent-holder may persist in extracting rents indefinitely.

# CHAPTER SIX

# The
# Decentralized
# Software Market

The world of software engineering is in no way restricted to software companies. Beyond Microsoft or thousands of smaller software vendors, almost every corporation in the world keeps a stable of programmers in the basement to write little scripts that move the company's e-mail and make the "add to cart" button do what it should. I am a programmer because I write simulations and statistical analyses. Even you are a software programmer if you use the Record Macro feature of your spreadsheet or word processor.

The variety in types of software producers engenders two distinct methods of pricing software. One, *shrink-wrap pricing*, derives from more ephemeral markets: software is sold by the unit (packaged in shrink-wrapped boxes, for example) at a per unit cost. The other, *labor-oriented pricing*, follows from an hourly wage or an annual salary paid to people in the basement who write code. To give a music analogy: a band may record an album in the studio and then charge for each copy of the recording, or it can be paid for playing a live gig, and then audience members can bootleg the concert and listen at home for free. Both are viable means of making recordings for the public and money for the band.

The latest accounting from the Bureau of Economic Analysis divides the software market into three parts: retail, consultants, and in-house, which are evenly split in the U.S. economy. Of the $232.5 billion spent on software in 2002, 32.6 percent bought prepackaged programs, 36.4 percent custom-built ones, and 31.0 percent software written in-house.[1] Since patent law is built around traditional products that are much more homogeneous, it is worth considering what will happen when the law for primarily product-oriented markets (such as drugs, machinery, and materials) is applied to a market that is one-third product oriented, one-third service oriented, and one-third a mix of the two.

## Comparative Advantage and the Programmers in the Basement

A good company, according to the management self-help books, stays focused on its core functions. If a company is good at making orange juice, it does not digress into selling autos, even if the owner knows an awful lot about cars. But any business of more than a few people, regardless of its actual purpose, will need word processors, an accounting and inventory system attached to a database, a website, e-mail, and somewhere from one person to an entire department to take care of all that software.

By contrast, no companies have a drug manufacturer in the basement to make sure that the accounting department has all the Prozac it needs to function smoothly, and if the accountants find that off-the-shelf Prozac does not quite work, they cannot hire a chemist to hack, patch, or customize Prozac for the company's specialized needs. Yet no matter how much work is shifted to Microsoft, SAP, or other contractors, it will always come down to the in-house information technology (IT) department to make sure the company's software is installed and working properly. Although they are often invisible (until something breaks), the people in the basement are an integral part of the software industry.

### The Communists Are Coming!

What happens to the software in the basement after it is written? Most software is so entirely location and task specific that it is used once and forgotten. Sometimes, however, it is so useful and new that the programmers in the basement form a company and start selling CDs—in fact, this is how a number of shrink-wrapped software products started out: for

---

1. By revenue; U.S. Department of Commerce, Bureau of Economic Analysis, "Recognition of Business and Government Expenditure for Software as Investment: Methodology and Quantitative Impacts, 1959–98" (www.bea.gov/bea/papers/software.pdf). Updated with 2002 data at www.bea.gov/bea/papers/table11.xls.

example, the SABRE flight reservation system (originally written at American Airlines, now owned by SABRE Holdings), the CADAM design program (originally from Lockheed, now owned by CADAM, Inc.), the Eudora e-mail client (written at and used by the University of Illinois, now owned by Qualcomm), or GAMS mathematical modeling software (written at the World Bank, now owned by GAMS Development).

With increasing frequency, software is also being given away to anyone who asks. Locking down a piece of software to license and sell it is just not worth the effort in the vast majority of cases—if a company has a comparative advantage in selling insurance or sofas, what business does it have in software consulting? It may have some great programmers in the basement, but hiring a sales team, getting the legal department up to speed on software licensing, and finding new ways to distribute software instead of sofas is a stretch far beyond the company's primary comparative advantage.

If a company is not hoping to make big profits from a piece of software, its best bet is to go to the other extreme and open the code base entirely, allowing for free and open collaboration. There are programmers in hundreds of basements who need a good database client. One writes the core of a database client and puts all the code out for inspection. Then another programmer, ensconced in another basement, finds that the code does what her company needs but has a few bugs, which she fixes. In another basement, another wage slave finds that the code works well, except it is missing support for BLOBs (binary large objects), so she adds that. The process continues, as everybody contributes the feature that makes the code perfect in their eyes, until—for the time needed to write a few functions—everyone has a full-featured and well-tested database.

Such collaboration in software dates back to when there were a handful of computers in the United States and a small community of programmers who knew how to work them. Since then collaboration has become infinitely easier thanks to the Internet.[2] Although some would claim that the collaborative system is the latest trend, shrink-wrapped software sold at unit cost is the new business model in this field.

It may sound like wishful thinking, but the collaborative method has produced some very heavy-duty software. As of October 2005,

---

2. A personal account of this history is given in the biography of Richard Stallman (Williams 2002), a vocal advocate of the collaborative method.

69.89 percent of websites use Apache, a free program developed in about the same manner as just described.[3] As well as web pages, one's e-mail probably arrives via collaborative software (either Sendmail or IBM-sponsored Postfix), and all the computers involved found each other via the Internet addressing program that most servers use, Berkeley Internet Name Daemon (BIND), which is also free software. Such software goes by a variety of names, including free software, libre software, open-source software, or the catch-all FLOSS.[4]

A report assessing the popularity of FLOSS in three European countries has found some variation in its use: only 18 percent of establishments in Sweden use some sort of open-source software; 31 percent do so in the United Kingdom; and 44 percent do in Germany.[5] Sectors also vary greatly in this regard, with public sector organizations using more open-source software than those in the private sector.

Thirty-six percent of the companies surveyed agreed with the statement, "Our software developers are free to work on Open Source projects within their time at work," while 46 percent disagreed.[6] In other words, the plurality of companies insist that their employees' work remain the company's property, but a large percentage of for-profit enterprises allow some of their employees' work to be given away for free.

Open-source programmers are often characterized as hobbyists who are learning computer science or just having fun with pet projects of no

---

3. Netcraft 2005 Web Server Survey (news.netcraft.com/archives/web_server_survey. html). Microsoft's IIS comes in second, with a 20.55 percent share. A website is defined as one host name.

4. The naming of this type of software hints at some massive infighting among FLOSS advocates, even though they agree on virtually everything else. In a recent interview ("Thus Spake Stallman," *Slashdot*, May 1, 2000 [slashdot.org/interviews/00/05/01/1052216. shtml]), Richard Stallman, founder of the Free Software Foundation, takes pains to point out that "I am not affiliated with the Open Source Movement. I founded the Free Software Movement." He reserves especial vitriol for the writing of leading open-source advocate Eric S. Raymond, perhaps because Raymond has said of Stallman: "As an evangelist to the mainstream, he's been one fifteen-year long continuous disaster" (www.catb.org/~esr/ writings/shut-up-and-show-them.html). The naming fight underscores the idea that the software should be free of licensing restrictions ("free as in speech") rather than simply free of cost ("free as in beer"). The term FLOSS is a pleasing compromise because it forms a common, albeit irrelevant, word from all of the options. Here, I refer to FLOSS as "open-source" software because I think it sounds nicer and also use the term "collaborative software" to refer to the means of producing software in a decentralized manner even when the output is not free or open.

5. International Institute of Infonomics (2004).

6. International Institute of Infonomics (2004, pt. I, sec. 4.1).

real significance. Although some of them would certainly meet that description, a reported 29 percent of Europe's open-source programmers are paid for developing free software at work, and 24 percent are not paid for doing so but do it on company time anyway.[7] Add to this the 17 percent of developers who are students, and only a few remain who are developing open-source software in their spare time.[8] The European Commission study states that "the development of Open Source/Free Software is not at all a matter of leisure 'work' at home. Ninety-five percent of the sample claim that they use OS/FS at work, school, or university."[9]

### Making Money on Free Software

A number of little companies use free software to make money. For example, IBM sells mainframes, but if it can throw in free software that makes its mainframes powerful web and e-mail servers, then it can move more metal. In a similar vein, Sun gives away Java. Another name on the list of success stories is Red Hat, which provides consulting services for corporations and creates neat packages of free software for consumers. Hans Reiser, designer of the best UNIX file system (the reiserfs), sells features: he has a to-do list of a dozen features that he wants to implement in his file system, but when the president of MP3.com offered him tens of thousands of dollars to implement a feature necessary for MP3.com business, he quickly obliged. MP3.com saved millions of dollars by switching to free software using Reiser's free file system, and Reiser profited from what he would have done anyway.[10]

Collaborative software is clearly a threat to the shrink-wrapped software market, because, as the saying goes, it has to compete with free. But for the labor-oriented side of the market, the wealth of ready-to-download software merely creates new opportunities.

### Free Software and Optimal Pricing

What does economic theory say about free software written by profit-maximizing firms? It says that this behavior is efficient. In a free and open market with many competitors, each unit of a good should be priced at the cost of producing that very unit (that is, the marginal cost). The first

7. Ghosh and others (2002).
8. International Institute of Infonomics (2004, pt. IV, sec. 2.3).
9. International Institute of Infonomics (2004, pt. IV, sec. 3.1).
10. Hans Reiser, speech at California Institute of Technology, November 14, 2002.

unit of software requires some amount of labor, and that needs to be compensated in full by paying the programmer a salary or wage. The second unit can be produced at basically no cost, since it only needs to be copied, so a zero price for the second unit and beyond is what the theory predicts and can be shown to be efficient.

Meanwhile, shrink-wrapped software is not priced by marginal cost, but closer to average cost—spend a million dollars making the first CD, then make ten thousand copies and charge $100 for each of them. Since vendors have a copyright on their work, their software will differ in enough ways from that of their competitors to allow them to charge well above marginal cost for their products.

In practice, of course, products are seldom priced at marginal cost. Few goods in this world are truly standardized, and even among those that are (corn of a certain grade, or government bond futures, for example), some units still sell at well above marginal cost. The amazing thing about open-source software, from the perspective of the theoretical economist, is that it *actually fits the theory*. Most markets experience problems that theory must ignore or explain away: inventories, shipping costs, transaction costs, massive up-front investments, and the risks those imply. Given such imperfections, it makes sense to correct them by imposing laws that would otherwise be suboptimal—a primary example being patent law, which solves the up-front investment problem. But collaborative software actually fits the models: transaction costs are nil, investment problems are solved without patents, and one can actually apply the theories that predict optimality without apology. For open-source software, patents solve an economic problem that had not existed to begin with.

### Open Source and Patents

Not only do patents have no value or relevance to open-source software, but they have the potential to be a significant hindrance. By definition, open-source software lacks a centralized body through which to obtain patents, not to mention lawyers to defend against patent threats (although both IBM and Sun made limited pledges to support open-source authors in some patent-related issues, and even Lloyd's of London intends to sell liability insurance for servers running open-source software).[11] Adobe can sue Macromedia and vice versa, and both can afford

11. Other companies that have made patent pledges include Computer Associates, Nokia, Novell, and Red Hat. Robin Cover, ed., "Open Source Development Labs (OSDL)

to hire lawyers to keep them in business, but if anyone were to sue a collaborative project that does not have a patron backing it, the project would have no choice but to shut down.

The collaborative system depends on the source being open to all and making sure that everyone is free to modify the code. People who intend the code to be collaborative have an ingenious method of making it so: they copyright the code and claim complete control over its use. Then, in licensing out the code, they explicitly specify that users are free to redistribute or modify the code as they see fit, provided they do not impose their own restrictions. Although there are dozens of such contracts to choose from, the standard one delineating these rules is the GNU General Public License (GPL), where GNU stands for GNU's Not Unix.

Here is the key message from the GPL:[12] "This program is free software; you can redistribute it and/or modify it under the terms of the GNU General Public License." How would this work if some portion of the code were patented? If the patent-holder charges a licensing fee, the software cannot be costless any more. If the software can be freely redistributed, the patent-holder must give up his or her right to limit distribution. Since the software can be reworked into other applications, the patent-holder even gives up the right to redistribution in a potentially wide range of applications. Clearly, any patent-holder who wants to retain any vestige of control would not consent to a patent being used in GPLed code.

The GPL explicitly acknowledges that if a claim is asserted for patented code in a project, the project must shut down as a public endeavor: "If a patent license would not permit royalty-free redistributon of the Program by all those who receive copies directly or indirectly through you, then the only way you could satisfy both it and this License would be to refrain entirely from distribution of the Program." In short, patents and collaborative software cannot coexist, and if the two collide, patents win.

Collaborative software does have one advantage over patents. If a patent-holder threatens to shut down a collaborative project, the entire

Announces Patent Commons Project," Cover Pages, August 10, 2005 (http://xml.cover-pages.org/ni2005-08-10-a.html). Gavin Clarke, "Lloyd's Taking on Open Source IP Risk," The Register, August 12, 2005 (www.theregister.co.uk/2005/08/12/opensource_indemnification); "IBM Statement of Non-Assertion of Named Patents against OSS" (www.ibm.com/ibm/licensing/patents/pledgedpatents.pdf); Stephen Shankland, "Sun: Patent Use OK beyond Solaris Project," Cnet News, January 31, 2005 (news.com.com/Sun+Patent+use+OK+beyond+Solaris+project/2100-7344_3-5557658. html).
    12. Version 2 (1991).

project may shift to finding prior art that would invalidate the patent. With hundreds of people from diverse parts of the computer science world all focusing on searching for prior art, the odds are very high that something will turn up. The Electronic Frontier Foundation has used this strategy to locate prior art about items in its list of the worst software patents.[13]

This approach still relies on a great deal of publicity, so if a specialized project receives a cease-and-desist letter or there is a flood of patent claims throughout the open-source community, the required critical mass of eyeballs required to find good prior art may not be reached. Every web designer in the world could probably contribute something to a prior art search pertaining to Amazon's infamous patent 5,960,411, on one-click purchasing. But if the GNU Scientific Library gets a takedown notice for violating one of the fast Fourier transform patents (see page 63), a far smaller population could come to the GSL's support.[14]

Even if a community of users find prior art immediately, it still needs to be ruled upon by the courts or the U.S. Patent and Trade Office (USPTO), which would take months (in Internet Time, several centuries) and may still fail on the details. Many users would be too risk-averse to wait for the ruling and would stop using the technology until clarity is restored.

Much has been made of security risks to the Internet and the potential havoc a terrorist could cause by a well-placed worm, virus, or technical glitch that might bring down large parts of the network. But here is the surest and simplest way to shut down the Internet: find a function or data structure in BIND or Apache that is under the scope of a patent, hire a lawyer, and start suing as many people as possible. For BIND especially, there are few alternatives, and switching is technically difficult—and who knows whether the alternatives are patent-free?

Microsoft has even thrown out a few warnings that such lawsuits are inevitable for users of open source software.[15] Fortunately, the company

13. The Electronic Frontier Foundation's Patent Busting Project, at eff.org/patent/.

14. This is not to say that the FFT patents are a special interest issue: not many people may know how to calculate FFTs, but most cell phones, DVD players, and cable boxes do. A disclaimer: when I wrote this sentence, I had in mind the maintainers of the GSL. But the description of how open-source software can benefit all involved earlier in this chapter was so persuasive that I have since initiated an open-source project based on the statistical functions I use in my own work (see apophenia.info). Therefore, the problem of patent exposure now applies to me directly.

15. John Lettice, "Use Linux and You *Will* Be Sued, Ballmer Tells Government," *The Register,* November 2004 (www.theregister.co.uk/2004/11/18/ballmer_linux_lawsuits/).

provides its own operating system and server software (IIS on Windows), which risk-averse companies can use to replace Apache on Linux, and provides indemnification protection by (and from) Microsoft's legal department.[16] Indeed, at least one case (*J2 Global Communications* v. *Mijanda, Inc.*) has cropped up over alleged patent infringement by open-source software used by the defendant.[17]

Even a single function could lead to a patent suit, so lawsuit-averse programmers had best purchase function libraries from vendors instead of writing their own and glue them together using a purchased copy of Microsoft's Visual Studio instead of a freely downloaded copy of the GNU Compiler Collection. Perhaps the best bet is to simply stop writing programs entirely and purchase all software from those centralized vendors who own the patent thickets that can provide indemnification.

At one time, the labor market and the shrink-wrap market were in a balanced relationship: software companies sold their goods to the labor-oriented side, which applied them to their projects, and everybody made money. But now that there is a well-established and tested mechanism to allow the labor-oriented side to incrementally build the operating system and desktop-level software that is the specialty of the shrink-wrap vendor, the goods-oriented side of the couple has been spurned. It is only natural that the goods-oriented side would use all of the weapons available to ensure that the labor side remains bound to the union.

## Decentralization

Another way to cast the difference between the goods-oriented and labor-oriented market is to say that the labor-oriented market is massively decentralized. On one hand, there are only a few tractor companies, which maintain a full-time staff of the best and brightest. If those central repositories of mechanical knowledge are not well supported, the tractor arts cannot advance. There may be some inventive tinkerers cobbling

16. Ina Fried, "Microsoft to Back Customers in Infringement Cases," ZDNet, November 10, 2004 (http://news.zdnet.com/2100-3513_22-5445868.html).

17. Pamela Jones, "Patent Lawsuits That Involve FOSS," *Groklaw*, August 10, 2005 (www.groklaw.net/article.php?story=2005080914234645). Normally, using a patented device is *contributory infringement*, which can be prosecuted in a manner similar to direct infringement. But recall Judge Rich's opinion in *In re Alappat* (chapter 3): to load a program onto a computer is to build a new machine, meaning that Mijada is directly infringing the patent, even though its employees may not have written a single line of the open-source program that is the core of the infringement claims.

together contraptions outside of these companies, but the vast majority of tractor technology is developed and supported by tractor vendors. On the other hand, every basement of every corporation has its program-mers, and they are producing fully operable software. If I want a program to do any given function, say, convert document formats or implement a database, dozens or even hundreds of viable options are at my disposal, only a fraction of which were written by people at software companies.

The abundance of languages and libraries helps: for any given task, there are so many tools already in existence that a designer can have a basic running program rather quickly. A wealth of database engines are lying around just for the taking, waiting to be built into larger devices; the same certainly could not be said of tractor engines.

The structure of software also makes decentralized programming easy. So long as he does not change the function's interface, a program-mer can tweak, debug, and optimize the function implementation all he wants without affecting the other parts of the project that use the func-tion. This means that after the overall high-level design is done, there is little or no benefit to having all of the programmers in one place. Of course, the fact that the product can be e-mailed instantaneously at zero cost helps as well.

I stress this decentralization because some pro-patent authors believe patent difficulties can be attributed entirely to the relationship between patents and open-source software. Since open-source advocates are mere hobbyists on the fringe, they reason, one can safely ignore them and focus policy on the vendors of software. As already mentioned, open-source software is neither written primarily by hobbyists nor produced on the fringe. Even so, the central problem is not about open source, but about centralized versus decentralized production. The best examples of decen-tralized production are indeed open source—the Linux kernel was writ-ten by 418 programmers from 35 countries, on every continent but Antarctica—but even the companies with a no-open-source policy have programmers in the basement working full time on code and software.[18]

If a technology needs a centralized group to help it advance, then it makes sense to design a mechanism to support those few specialized experts who push forward the frontiers. In such a field, the patent-thicket

18. Ilkka Tuomi, "Evolution of the Linux Credits File: Methodological Challenges and Reference Data for Open Source Research," June 2004 (www.firstmonday.dk/issues/issue9_6/tuomi/). Data based on kernel 2.4.25, released July 2002.

problem is not a problem because there are only a few actors in the business, so the transaction costs of negotiating exchanges are low.

But this story is entirely removed from the reality of software. A third of the industry consists of centralized organizations that only write software while the rest is largely a decentralized body of workers supporting themselves and their innovations through immediate, direct application rather than waiting to put out a product in the near future. As far as Coasian arguments about transaction costs are concerned, this is absolutely the worst case, since buyers and sellers are distributed across the planet. Because every patent is unique, there is no easy way to create a simple market to make patent trading cheap.

The rule that independent invention is not a defense in infringement claims makes sense in a centralized industry. Patents are public record, and it is reasonable to assume that every tractor manufacturer is exerting some effort to watch every other such manufacturer. In the decentralized software industry, this does not make any sense at all: should the sofa company spend time and effort on monitoring Microsoft and Novell's patent portfolio? Add in the software patent search problems from chapter 5, and the assumption that everyone has full knowledge of the patent playing field becomes still more tenuous.

In short, patents in a decentralized market are Coase's worst nightmare: every player needs to expend vast quantities searching for the owner of every part of every program, meaning transaction costs piled upon transaction costs. These costs will always exist in every field, but they are magnified in a dense, decentralized network of actors.

Centralizing the patent search process (by hiring centralized full-time patent search firms to support the decentralized programmers) will not help much: searchers will still have to check every computational nut and bolt, and owing to the joys of mathematical abstraction, hundreds of patents like the singular value decomposition patent apply to hundreds of different fields. Because any Turing machine can be applied to any effectively computable problem, computer science itself is a dense network of concepts, each one a step or two away from virtually every other. To do a proper search, then, one would have to check almost every prior use of a Turing machine: in all, 170,000 patents and counting.

As an aside, the political landscape of software is a manifestation of the *collective action problem*: a centralized group that stands to gain significantly from a policy will lobby more vehemently than a decentralized group of many people who all stand to lose from the policy, and so inefficient political decisions are often made to please the most concentrated and vocal interests.[19] At the height of the European debate, centralized producers with large patent portfolios such as Adobe, Cisco Systems, IBM, and Microsoft spent a great many resources on lobbying the EU's decisionmakers.

The patent problems discussed in this chapter are not about open source; they are about decentralization. Software design was decentralized before open source became mainstream, and at least a third of the market, including a large subportion that does not open its source, remains decentralized. Patents were not designed to cover goods produced by thousands of companies that do not even work in the industry in question. There are many reasons to believe that they are not as good a fit for a massively decentralized system as for traditional centralized systems of production.

## How Patents Affect the Bifurcated Market

Patents primarily benefit the authors of shrink-wrapped software. Returning to the music metaphor, the band that makes its money playing gigs needs no IP protection. If fans do not pay at the door, they will not hear the music. The band that focuses on CD sales depends heavily on IP protection, since copies of its CDs are near-perfect substitutes for the originals. Similarly, the provider of a software product needs to differentiate his from that of others in order to charge a unit price greater than the near-zero unit cost. Copyright is sufficient for this, but as discussed in chapter 5, patents as they exist today are so broad that a patent-owner can carve out sole ownership of a much larger part of the market than a copyright-owner could. Meanwhile, a strictly labor-oriented employee is more indifferent to IP protection: if the company does not pay at the door, then the programmer will withhold his or her labor—no IP required.

As already mentioned, patents make the most sense and provide the most economic benefit in a system built around a few centralized vendors of goods. Conversely, they make no sense at all in the context of a decentralized network of laborers—especially if everyone has already found incentive to innovate in the need to do his or her own job better.

In real life, of course, the class of programmers does not bifurcate into those who provide only shrink-wrapped software and those who provide

19. For the classic description of the problem, see Olson (1971).

only day-to-day labor, but includes people whose work falls all along the range. In the middle are a variety of consultants, who typically offer both software (either off the shelf or custom made) and implementation services. To the extent that they differentiate themselves through their unique software, patents may help; to the extent that they differentiate through high-quality labor, patents are irrelevant.

Just as some bar bands prefer to strictly control bootleg recordings and profit from their sale, labor-oriented providers may be able to profit from controlling the software they produce. In the context here, there is potential for a labor-oriented programmer to turn into a product-oriented programmer. However, recall the matter of comparative advantage: the sofa company is not oriented toward software sales or software patent licensing, and reorienting the business would be costly. Meanwhile, vendors of shrink-wrapped software know the software market and need to make little or no extension to the main business to apply for and license software patents. In short, software patents are designed for and can help shrink-wrap vendors but do nothing for the labor-oriented sector—except to the extent that labor-oriented workers are or could become shrink-wrap vendors as well.

## The Future of Software

Allow me to make my predictions for the future of the software market. Computer services overall will continue to expand, while the market for shrink-wrapped software will become a smaller part of the equation, and the market for programming labor will expand. Of course, well-written shrink-wrapped software will always have a place in retail. Apple has shown that there is much to be said for having a professional design team working on the look and feel of a product, while authors of open-source and task-specific software are famous for poor graphic design. The open-source code base is constantly expanding, but that is no help here: although programs written in the mid-1980s often work perfectly today, goods that have not had a design overhaul since then look terrible to modern eyes.[20] Retail firms that put their effort into a good user interface will always have a market.

20. The open-source Athena widget set comes to mind.

Since consumers care much more about how their software looks and feels than database maintainers do, much of the demand is on the consumer side rather than the enterprise side. If nothing else, there is the games market: gamers have an insatiable desire for the faster, flashier, and newer items. However, games have no corporate clientele (at least not while the boss is watching), so they will never garner the hourly wage programmers, and open-source hobbyists have never been able to develop the critical mass of people necessary to put together the art, storyline, game play, and rendering needed to make a top-notch game.[21] Even so, gaming software is not just small change: sales in 2004 totaled $7.3 billion.[22]

There is more money yet in business software that nonprogrammers use (such as word processors and spreadsheets), which falls somewhere between the two extremes of beautiful games and ugly-but-efficient back ends. On the one hand, efficiency matters, but on the other, office workers are still human beings, and if they are going to spend a third of every twenty-four hours staring at a computer screen, it may as well look nice. In this range, things could go either way. To date, shrink-wrapped software has won out, because of aesthetic considerations and a strong focus on ease of initial use. But it does not have to be this way: the Department of Defense could hire programmers to add eye candy to OpenOffice.org (a collaboratively written office suite), and may still save money over licensing Microsoft Word.

Collaborative software is only getting better. OpenOffice.org is already more than sufficient for writing letters and balancing a home user's checkbook in a spreadsheet, and for all but the most demanding business uses. Even the French national police force uses this software on its 80,000 PCs.[23] The code base for OpenOffice.org will not disappear. If anything, the percentage of people who download free software that meets their

21. Sorry, Linux fans, but Tux Racer does not cut it.

22. Entertainment Software Association, "Computer and Video Game Software Sales Reach Record $7.3 Billion in 2004," *Yahoo! Finance*, January 26, 2005 (biz.yahoo.com/bw/050126/265772_1.html). For comparison, Microsoft's 2004 annual report lists $36.8 billion in sales.

23. "Le Gendarme et OpenOffice," Toolinux, January 16, 2004 (www.toolinux.com/news/logiciels/le_gendarme_et_openoffice_ar5768.html). "French Police to Switch to OpenOffice," Heise Online, January 18, 2004 (www.heise.de/english/newsticker/news/55253).

needs is likely to expand in comparison with the percentage who spend a few hundred dollars on an office suite that does a little more and comes with animated characters. People prefer familiar, tested software, which currently means proprietary products, but companies such as Google and municipalities such as the State of Massachusetts are using open-source software, so the getting-acquainted phase has already begun. I expect that five years from now, collaborative software will be as familiar as the common brand names of today. This is a looming threat for the shrink-wrap market, but neither a plus nor a minus for the labor market.

On the consumer side, there is only so much that users need a word processor to do. Unless users can be persuaded to upgrade on a regular basis, software may be a one-time investment. For example, I have many friends who use Windows 95. They admit it with shame, since the name clearly indicates that the software is a decade old. Yet it still meets their needs and they see no value in the expense of upgrading. At the same time, things always break, so individuals and companies will need IT professionals on hand long after the software licenses have been paid for. I still get calls from my friends with Windows 95, since problems continue to crop up at a regular pace. By contrast, business computing needs are complex. Corporations are no longer satisfied with a straightforward personnel database—they want one that automatically makes hiring decisions the way the vice president would make them, that integrates seamlessly with the accounting database, and that has an interface on the company's website. None of these things can be pulled out of a box; a programmer who knows the company will have to be hired to implement them.

Authors of retail software can be located in Seattle, India, or anywhere in between. As noted earlier, any competent programmer can implement any sufficiently detailed interface design, although a consultant hired to design the interface for a company is very likely to be on site, getting the lay of the company's virtual land. With increasing outsourcing and off-shoring (today's software market buzzwords), the number of domestic programmers writing shrink-wrapped software will decrease, but there will be less effect on the domestic programmers writing customized software. For all of these reasons, I foresee slower growth or even some contraction for shrink-wrapped software in the near future, whereas the market for custom programming labor will expand in close proportion to the increasing ubiquity and complexity of computing.

## *Back to Patents*

Patents favor the shrink-wrap market, which is the segment of the market likely to experience a decline. In this context, software patent laws are among those that economists despise most: namely, laws that artificially prop up an industry in decline. Like a spurned lover, the centralized vendors will fight to keep their portion of the market. Stronger patent laws to bear down on decentralized labor are a primary weapon in the fight.

If the market does not stay as it is today but shifts further from the per unit model toward the labor model, it is hard to predict whether the total number of programmers will rise or fall. Certainly, the information technology sector as a whole is not likely to suffer. On a more abstract level, free software or task-specific software can be expected to add as much or more value than shrink-wrapped software, and authors in the software labor market are likely to match or outdo software vendors when it comes to innovativeness.

From the perspective of society, and even the software industry as a whole, there is no need to protect the shrink-wrap segment of the market, or to change the rules to favor it over the labor-oriented segment. Yet that is exactly what software patents do, at the cost of hundreds of millions of dollars wasted in litigation.

# CHAPTER SEVEN

# Interoperability

Interoperability refers to the ability of one vendor's products to work with the data or interface from another vendor's products. Suppose that DBA Corp. writes a suite of programs to create databases, with a back end to do the bookkeeping and a front end to enter data. Then DBB Corp. writes a new front end that can read, write, and modify DBA-formatted files—and that has animated characters and thus sells much better than DBA Corp.'s front end. DBA Corp. had intended to sell both front and back ends and perhaps had priced its back end cheaply in the hopes of making money selling thousands of front ends. Now that people can buy a DBA back end but have the choice of a DBB front end, DBA has lost its revenues from front ends, while DBB has profited from DBA's engineering effort in designing its database format.

In a sense, protecting interoperability is a variant of the breadth question (see chapter 2). If DBA Corp.'s back end is sufficiently innovative to merit intellectual property (IP) protection, should that protection be broad enough to cover its front end as well? Three types of IP law relate to interoperability: the regulations covering patents, copyright, and an entirely new type of IP derived from the Digital Millennium Copyright Act (DMCA). One must ask whether these IP laws strike the correct balance between the economic benefits of having an abundance of interoperable software and the incentives needed to keep standard writers working.

Interoperability is an issue in any of a number of fields, but more so for software, *all* of which must interoperate with comparable products like DBA's back end or the operating system or assembly language whose back the program rests on. For many physical goods, interoperability simply means that tab A must be the right width to fit into slot B, but software interoperability depends on implementing interfaces that often take hundreds of pages to specify; hence the owner of the interface has abundant opportunity to claim copyright or patent infringement by the designer of the interoperating software. Further, the concept of encryption makes sense only in the context of data, so the encryption-oriented DMCA applies only to software.

## Leveraging the Dominant Library

One class of standards includes the de facto standard established by a piece of software having the lion's share of the market, such as Microsoft's desktop operating systems. Indeed, many of Microsoft's actions are perfect examples of a dominant player leveraging its dominance into greater profits by breaking interoperability between its products and those of others.

Consider the system that programmers have developed to collect sets of useful functions in function libraries to facilitate the writing of advanced code (see chapter 3). Anyone who wants to run the high-level program needs both the program itself and all the function libraries supporting it. Outside of the most basic, ANSI-regulated libraries, there are few standard libraries in the world. Most large software companies have written their own from scratch. Microsoft and Apple both have a library of functions to do the accounting required to draw windows on the user's screen: the Microsoft library has a `CreateWindow` function while the MacOS library has a `CreateNewWindow` function. A programmer wanting to write for both systems would have to have a version of the program that used `CreateWindow` and another that used `CreateNewWindow`. By itself, this one renaming is a minor annoyance, but factor in the thousands of additional changes that need to be made—some fundamental to the structure of the typical program—and the cost of writing a program for both libraries can approach double the cost of writing the program for just one.

It so happens that Microsoft Windows is installed on about 94 percent of the world's desktop computers, meaning that Microsoft's preferred function libraries are preinstalled on 94 percent of the world's desktop PCs.[1] Since writing a program for Windows and MacOS can be almost like writing the same program twice, a company with limited resources must choose between the two—and since MacOS has about a 3 percent desktop market share, it is easy to decide which libraries to write around first.[2]

Sun Microsystems had an idea for producing a new set of libraries that could run on Microsoft's, Apple's, and its own system without modification. Its programmers would write implementations for all the operating systems and guarantee that the interface is the same in all cases. Coders could write once for Sun's interface, and users could run the program anywhere.

This marked the genesis of the Java language. It was implemented through a virtual machine, which could understand programs written using Sun's standard Java header files. Sun then persuaded Netscape, Inc. to include a Java virtual machine in the Netscape Navigator web browser. The hope was that people would be able to use the browser to download programs written in Java and run those programs regardless of the operating system their computer was running.

Sun's agenda here is clear: with more programs written around Java libraries instead of Windows libraries, people would be more likely to buy Sun hardware. If programmers do not have to choose whether to write only for Windows or expend great effort rewriting for both Windows and Mac, then the dominance of Windows would not be so relevant any more, and Microsoft's operating system, with its proprietary libraries and 94 percent market share, would become a much less valuable property. Microsoft did not like this prospect and so gave away Internet Explorer in an effort to prevent people from downloading Netscape and its Java virtual machine. This attempt to halt Java was one of the key points of contention in the antitrust action the Department of Justice brought against Microsoft.[3]

As well as trying to keep users from downloading Netscape, Microsoft had a second solution that was a bit more insidious: it invented its own version of Java, which it included with Internet Explorer. This version was

1. As of late 2002. IDC survey, cited in Laura Rohde, "Microsoft Dominance of OS Market Grows, IDC Study Says," *MacCentral*, October 8, 2003 (maccentral.macworld.com/news/2003/10/08/osmarket/).
2. Rohde (2003).
3. Gilbert and Katz (2002).

*almost* like Sun's Java, but the interface was different enough that it created the same old dilemma: whether to write around the Sun libraries or the Microsoft libraries. Now that the "write once, run everywhere" appeal of Java was lost, the language never gained the hoped-for popularity.

Novell, owner of the once-dominant WordPerfect word processor, had a similar complaint in *Novell* v. *Microsoft*:[4]

> 74. In an email dated October 3, 1994, . . . Bill Gates ordered his top executives to retract the documentation of the browsing [interface for Windows 95], but only until Microsoft's own developers of the Office suite of applications had sufficient time to work with the hidden extensions to build an insurmountable advantage over competitors such as WordPerfect. . . .
>
> 76. . . . Novell had no choice but to spend more than a year recreating the functionality of Windows' integrated browsing functions. As Gates knew and intended, withdrawing the documentation of the browsing APIs caused Novell, in Microsoft's own words, to re-invent the wheel and divert resources from innovations on behalf of consumers. Microsoft's applications developers, by contrast, had unfettered access to the integrated browsing extensions all along.

As these examples show, the power to break interoperability is not to be taken lightly. The question of whether Microsoft's refusal to cooperate with Java and WordPerfect was a violation of antitrust law is beyond the scope of this book.[5] The central concern here is the extent to which government should provide IP protection for the interfaces needed for interoperability. Since interoperability disputes like these are so common, it is worth considering the balance between fostering innovation and the inefficiency of monopolies in their context.

---

4. Novell complaint in *Novell* v. *Microsoft* (www.novell.com/news/press/archive/2004/11/complaint.pdf).

5. Even if an organization has the exclusive rights granted by a patent, it still cannot use them to engage in activities that transgress antitrust law. In an eminently quotable ruling from *United States* v. *Microsoft,* the appellate court scolded Microsoft for making such a claim: "The company claims an absolute and unfettered right to use its intellectual property as it wishes: 'if intellectual property rights have been lawfully acquired,' it says, then 'their subsequent exercise cannot give rise to antitrust liability.' Appellant's Opening Br. at 105. That is no more correct than the proposition that use of one's personal property, such as a baseball bat, cannot give rise to tort liability. As the Federal Circuit succinctly stated: 'Intellectual property rights do not confer a privilege to violate the antitrust laws.'" *United States* v. *Microsoft Corp.,* 253 F.3d 34, 63 (D.C. Cir. 2001).

## Value versus Price

A competing interoperable product has the interesting effect of both making the original product more valuable (because it now interoperates with a wider range of other goods) and forcing its price—and possibly its profits—downward. In such a situation, one cannot resort to the standard economic theories stating that the market will find the optimum for the society: the dominant player's most profitable strategy may be to destroy value by breaking interoperability between its goods and those of competitors.

As the literature documents, when a monopolist decides to bundle goods together rather than price them independently, bundling is generally great for the monopolist but bad for everyone else.[6] Tom Palfrey, currently at Princeton University, has pointed out: "Because the seller earns greatest profit by bundling all goods, a profit maximizing seller will pick the *worst* bundling decision both from the point of view of buyers and in welfare terms."[7] In the case of interoperating software, the originator of the system has no natural monopoly because competitors can enter and force the originator to unbundle its product. However, patents on the interface between the two would grant the originator the right to not unbundle.

Noninteroperability creates the famous lock-in problem: if everyone wants to imitate those who came before, the first to appear on the market has a strong advantage, and once one product or another is dominant, new buyers can be expected to simply stop evaluating the options and go with the most popular. Because new buyers add no new information, and because it is difficult for the society as a whole to switch to another option, the market may become locked in an inefficient equilibrium.[8] But if the two options become interoperable, people will feel a correspondingly weaker need to imitate others. Given such a shift, the probability that the society will find itself in the inefficient equilibrium will correspondingly decrease.[9] So what good is lock-in? It allows for creative price lists.

Recall the discussion from chapter 2, which concluded that good IP protection is sufficient to allow the original researcher to recoup the costs

6. See, for example, Bakos and Brynjolfsson (1999) and Chen (1997).
7. Palfrey (1983, p. 473).
8. Bikhchandani, Hirshleifer, and Welch (1992).
9. Brock and Durlauf (2001); Klemens (2003).

of research but does not go significantly beyond that point. In the case here, DBA Corp. had invested $R$ dollars in research for its system, which it needs to recover via higher prices to its products. It could split the costs, adding half of $R$ to the price of the front end and half to the back end, or it could add $R$ entirely to the cost of the back end. If there are lock-in effects to be taken advantage of, DBA Corp. may choose to price its back end cheaply, and then distribute the research costs $R$—and then some— among the cost of additional front ends.

As for DBB, its improvement was on the front end, while DBA Corp. had a back end that was unique or of sufficient quality to sell at a premium and use the profits to recoup some of its research costs. Given such a setup, there is simply no reason to give DBA Corp. protection on its front end. If competition from DBB Corp. forces DBA to price its front end exactly at cost, DBA can still make its money by pricing its back end to include research costs. However, DBA has lost out on its ability to invent new business models—of the three mentioned in the preceding paragraph, only one will work if DBA must price its front end at cost.

Note well that the existence of DBB's front end makes DBA's back end more valuable, and since there is no competition to push down prices, DBA will be able to price it higher. What if DBB Corp. also produces a competing back end? If the back end is of sufficient quality to surpass DBA's back end, then the entire interoperability issue is a moot point, since consumers can buy DBB's entire system. In every case, if DBA provides a back end of sufficient quality, it will be able to charge a premium for it—and a higher one because DBB's front end is on the market.

Business models abound that price the base of a system below cost or even give it away for free and then charge a premium for add-ons, such as the expensive ink for underpriced printers and the premium service contracts for free cellular phones. But it is difficult to argue that the only way in which the printer or cell phone business could possibly operate is if it could use a business model in which everything is priced either above or below its cost of production. The simple and direct method of pricing goods at their cost plus some premium if the item is unique or of superior quality works for most fields and is considered optimal by most economists.

Therefore protection of DBA's front end is not necessary for DBA Corp. to design good back ends—if it has a good back end, then people will pay a premium for it. The only benefit to giving DBA Corp. legal protection from interoperable competitors is that such protection facilitates creative price lists.

The first moral to the story is that distinct products should be evaluated separately. Even if the back end has no value unless it is used in combination with a front end (and vice versa), both back and front ends will sell for a positive price. The second moral is the same rule of thumb from prior chapters: there is no economic benefit to protecting the interface.

## The Standard Bearers

In contrast to the preceding examples, where one company produced a product that gained dominance and thus defined a de facto standard, there are countless efforts to create standards effectively from scratch, such as CORBA, SQL, CGI, MPI, BLAS, and a multitude of other acronyms that every programmer must deal with every day.[10] These standards are entirely lacking in IP protection.

A useful and tangible example is the Universal Serial Bus (USB) standard. Versions of most of the devices one would plug into a computer (mice, keyboards, cameras, scanners, and so on) plug into a USB port and therefore must have software that complies with USB standards. The standard is maintained by the USB Implementer's Forum, Inc. (USB-IF), and the standard itself is available as a free download from the forum's website (usb.org). The forum's financial support comes from a number of sources, one being a group of companies that recognize the value of consistent standards. These companies can also individually benefit by biasing the standards toward their engineers' comparative advantages, or by simply knowing the standards better than everyone else.

Revenue also derives from the use of the USB logo, which is a trademark of the forum and cannot be used without paying a licensing fee, currently $1,500. Before putting the logo on a product, vendors must also pay to have their devices tested for compliance with the standard by an approved testing lab.

There are such great benefits to designing and giving away good standards that different standards bodies often compete for dominance in a

10. For those who need their acronyms unfurled: the Common Object Request Broker Architecture is used for moving data between applications, Structured Query Language is for extracting information from databases, the Common Gateway Interface is for running applications on a web server, the Message Passing Interface is for running programs on multiple processors (also known as cluster or grid computing), and the Basic Linear Algebra Subprograms are a common interface for libraries of matrix algebra functions.

single field. The 1394 Trade Association, administrators of the IEEE 1394 standard (Firewire), competes closely with the USB-IF.

Apart from the trademarked logos, the entire business exists outside the realm of intellectual property protection. Since everyone is encouraged to use the standards, any patents on Firewire or USB that are controlled by the 1394 Trade Association or USB-IF are not enforced. The official documents themselves are copyrighted, but an author who wishes to write a *USB for Idiots* guide that covers the same information is free to do so.

As for what society needs to do to get an innovator to write good standards, it does not take much: there are abundant ways to profit from a good standard without government intervention of any sort. Of course, granting the innovator patents, copyrights, and other means of suing competitors out of business would motivate the standard-bearer to produce, but at an unnecessary cost to the rest of society and the economy, in relation to free-market means of producing standards.

The discussion now turns to the specific means of blocking interoperability. Patents would invoke the fact that (a hard drive on which is written) a data structure is patentable. Copyrights would follow the example of copyrights on a language and would rely on the words used in a data structure or standard. Using a more direct approach, the DMCA is clearly oriented toward breaking interoperability, regardless of its form.

## Patenting an Interface

The most common standards among patents are file formats: music is typically stored on a computer in WAV or MP3 format; plain text is usually in the ASCII format or one of many ISO formats; word processor documents are often stored in Microsoft Word's DOC format. As the reader will recall, a file format is a data structure written down outside the program (chapter 3), and the Court of Appeals for the Federal Circuit (CAFC) has ruled in *In re Lowry* that a hard drive having a novel data structure written on it is a patentable device (chapter 4). As a practical matter of current law, then, a dominant player may use patents to break interoperability.

Also, if Microsoft succeeds in patenting the DOC data structure used by its word processor, nobody will be able to write software compatible with Word without permission from Microsoft. Although Microsoft's patent application is primarily for the DOC format itself, some of the claims (see figure 3-2) are for a very broadly described program used to read files in such a format.[11] In accordance with the preceding discussion, if the format is not Microsoft's private property, then competing products and Word itself both become more valuable. However, Word would then have more competition, which might force Microsoft to lower its price.

But users do not pay for a nice file format; they pay for a good implementation that makes use of the format. If Word's file interface was displayed in skywriting over Silicon Valley, competitors would still have to expend the cost and effort to implement their word processors without additional information about Word's implementation. That is, the discussion from chapter 2 applies directly: it is the implementation, not the interface, where the lion's share of the effort and expense lies, so any protection granted should focus on the implementation.

Yet what if a program's primary innovation lies in its file format? This is clearly not the case for a word processor, as made evident by the fact that WordPerfect, StarOffice, and OpenOffice.org all know each other's formats and yet felt the need to reinvest in inventing their own format anyway. If, on the other hand, a program's primary innovation was its file format, then that program would be treading dangerously close to an innovative mathematical algorithm. Again, there are many reasons why allowing a patent on such a work is both aesthetically inappropriate and economically detrimental.

## Copyrighting an Interface

As described in chapter 3, programmers have invented hundreds of languages to facilitate their work. Function libraries have their own list of commands that one could execute, and those are verbs in a language. Even the mouse gestures and typed inputs to a user-level application are the semiotics of a highly specialized language.

Should a language be copyrightable subject material? This is not as salient an issue as the question of patents, because patents are currently in favor with the courts and USPTO and allow broader protections. But since many have proposed that code be protected by copyright instead of

11. Microsoft has stated that it will offer its XML formats via a royalty-free license to all takers; see Ken Fisher "Microsoft Patenting New Office XML Format," *Ars Technica*, January 26, 2004 (arstechnica.com/news.ars/post/20040126-3336.html). However, its past royalty-free licenses excluded open-source providers from using their technology. For example, the Apache Software Foundation said of Microsoft's royalty-free sender ID license: "We believe the current license is generally incompatible with open source, contrary to the prac-

patents, it is important to consider exactly how far the protection of an author's words should extend.

According to 17 U.S.C. §102 (b), "In no case does copyright protection for an original work of authorship extend to any idea, procedure, process, system, method of operation, concept, principle, or discovery, regardless of the form in which it is described, explained, illustrated, or embodied in such work." That is, the dictionary and the grammar textbook may readily be copyrighted, but the ideas expressed therein may not be. This is similar to the previous description of a good patent law: it covers the implementation of the idea, but not the idea itself.

However, even without reference to ideas, procedures, or the other conceptual ideas in §102, perhaps an interface can still be protected via its details of expression. If I invent words such as *mscorlib*, *stdio*, and *outgrabe*, may others use those words without my permission? If a program demands that anything it deals with use the word *outgrabe*, then copyrighting that word is an effective block on any sort of interoperation with the program.

### A Proliferation of Languages

For comparison, consider the cases in which people have invented a human-oriented language and claimed a copyright over the words in the language. Loglan, invented by James Cooke Brown from basic logical principles, was such a language. Brown claimed the language as his own, which induced legal squabbling with some of Loglan's supporters. Because of these difficulties, not to mention the logical errors found in the language, it branched into a variant version, Lojban, which now competes with the original language.[12]

Another such language is Klingon, spoken by a race of aliens on the *Star Trek* series and an ever-expanding group of devoted fans. The language has the support of the nonprofit Klingon Language Institute, and Pocket Books has published a paperback translation of *Hamlet*.[13] However, the

---

tice of open Internet standards, and specifically incompatible with the Apache License 2.0" (www. apache.org/foundation/docs/sender-id-position.html). Whether the details of its licensing of its XML format will exclude major competitors is yet to be seen.

12. The Logical Language Group, Inc., "Loglan and Lojban," 1991 (www.lojban.org/files/brochures/loglan.txt).

13. Information about the KLI is available at KLI.org. See also Shoen and the KLI (2000).

language itself is claimed (without challenge to date) as the property of Paramount Pictures, and Paramount claims that no works may be written in the language without its permission.

But Loglan and Klingon differ from the language described by a computing interface because they have little purpose but expression—they are purely creative. It is unclear whether the courts would support Paramount if a Klingon challenger were to appear; Paramount would likely argue that if the language were not the property of a single entity, the originators of the language might not have put so much effort into its improvement.

In contrast, the language of a computing interface has a specific purpose. For example, John Chambers of Bell Labs wrote the S programming language to provide a better way to describe statistical models. If he had not invested his effort into writing the grammar, nouns, and verbs of S, he would have had to use some less appropriate language for his statistical analyses. He wrote the language not expecting a profit, but as a new means of expression that would make his work easier.

When Donald Knuth of Stanford University became frustrated by the typesetting of his *Art of Programming*, he did what any reasonable programmer would do in such a situation: he wrote a typesetting language from scratch (named TEX). If he had not done so, he would have had to settle for a less appealing book.

Larry Wall, two-time winner of the International Obfuscated C Code Contest, was sick of UNIX system administration work: "Unix is like a toll road on which you have to stop every 50 feet to pay another nickel. But hey! You only feel 5 cents poorer each time."[14] Being such an excellent programmer, he wrote a new language named Perl to simplify the tasks he had to deal with every day. If he had not done so, he would still be paying out his metaphoric nickels.

Virtually every programming language has such a history, as do hundreds of libraries that also implement a specialized language. Necessity, not copyright, was the mother of these invented languages.

Having developed the language, the inventor will find the easiest way to protect it is never to share it. If a company develops a language well suited for writing a word processor (probably in the form of a library of functions), then it is under no obligation to make that language public, so

14. "The Timeline of Perl and Its Culture," version 3.0_0505 (history.perl.org/PerlTimeline.html).

other developers of word processors would not be able to free-ride on the original company's efforts.

Instead, at issue here are those languages that are entirely public. In the case of Microsoft's Word document format, the company has no choice but to make it public. To give a more salient example, Microsoft's .NET platform is an extensive set of standards, document-type definitions, and libraries. In the inclusive terminology I use here, it is a set of languages. It is intended to help programmers write portable programs quickly. Microsoft can include .NET libraries in its products so that users can run .NET-based programs without downloading new libraries for every new program. Since programmers need to know how to call the functions, how to structure their documents, and so on, the product must by definition be public.

Mono is an open-source implementation of the languages and specifications of the .NET platform. The authors' intent is to match Microsoft's interface exactly but implement the tools and libraries using entirely new code. Users could run programs written using Mono tools if they have .NET libraries on their computer.

As it is, Microsoft has made no complaints of copyright infringement against Mono's developers.[15] Moreover, it is unclear whether such a claim would hold up in court—but is this optimal? Should Microsoft be able to claim infringement of its copyright?

### The Options

If the courts allow these languages to be copyrighted, programmers can still look at the language, learn from the ideas embodied therein, and write a new language similar enough to embody the same concepts but also different enough to avoid copyright infringement. Those who were enamored of Loglan did this when they designed Lojban. An author who is enamored of Microsoft's window library may replace its `CreateWindow` function with a `CreateNewWindow` function. A few dozen such changes may be enough to eliminate the copyright threat.

The immediate outcome is a tower of Babel. Every dialect is *almost* close enough to match, but not quite, and therefore translators are required to massage one language until it looks like another. Inefficiency abounds. The problem is that copyright can only restrict the literal

---

15. There is some gossip about the potential for future patent issues, which is beyond the scope of this section. See www.mono-project.com/about/licensing.html.

implementation of the language, not the ideas embodied therein.[16] Here are the alternatives:

1. Allow broad copyrights on a language, covering every conceivable dialect.

2. Allow strict copyright on languages, covering only languages with exactly the same vocabulary and grammar.

3. Disallow copyrights on languages entirely.

Option 1 is in effect a patent on the underlying ideas that the language implements, which would violate §102 and suffers the same problems of overbreadth discussed in the context of patents. Further, it is impossible to enforce: is Catalan a dialect of Spanish or a separate language? Is Scheme a LISP dialect? Is Apple's `CreateNewWindow` function too much like Microsoft's `CreateWindow` function? Linguists and computer scientists have debated such questions for decades; I do not expect the courts to do much better.[17]

Option 2 is the most inefficient of all, since it does not prevent approximate imitation (as option 1 would) and it forces language writers to make themselves unnecessarily incompatible with each other (as option 3 would not). It does not protect the creator's work from imitation, only from compatible imitation.

Option 3 is by far the least of the three evils. Some will argue that it eliminates some incentives to write new languages, but as shown by the standard writers and the language authors, many others remain. The .NET platform consists of an interface of languages and specifications, but it is supported by an implementation consisting of copyrighted tools and libraries that programmers can use to write code compliant to .NET, and by copyrighted Microsoft documentation that defines its languages. The developers of Mono have had to start from scratch, writing new tools, new libraries, and new documentation. They face an immense task: writing a `CreateWindow` function is easy, but writing a `CreateWindow` function that works 100 percent like Microsoft's is much more difficult. To date, Mono's implementation of the .NET languages still does not quite work exactly like Microsoft's, so a developer who is concerned with strict adherence to Microsoft's standards will need to purchase Microsoft tools.

---

16. A reminder: patents protect only implementation, not ideas as well. Therefore, the same three options could hold for an economic discussion of the patenting of languages with little or no modification.

17. Some linguists define a language as a dialect with an army. Let us hope that this definition never applies to a programming language.

Even with no protection on the interface, Microsoft still has a market in selling implementations.

Before .NET, words like *P/Invoke* and *mscorlib* did not exist, just as before Lewis Carroll's "Jabberwocky," *brillig* and *bandersnatch* had not existed. But practically, economically, and even ethically, giving Carroll control over *brillig* and giving Microsoft control over *mscorlib* are very different. The creative force behind "Jabberwocky" lies in the words themselves, so if an imitator were to rewrite the poem replacing *brillig* with *midafternoon* and *bandersnatch* with *alligator*, the imitation would have no value. The creative force behind .NET is not the words at all: it is the structures and the ideas that inspired the language. Replacing *mscorlib* with *monocorlib* would have no effect on the underlying ideas and would produce a new imitation with exactly the same force, productivity, and salability as the original—except that it would be incompatible with .NET. Thus copyright protection on the programming language itself (in the form of a language proper, a library, or a standard) does not protect the fruits of the original creator's mind as copyright does in other contexts; instead it serves only to stifle those who hope to build upon the original work. The economically optimal breadth of copyright does not prevent interoperability.

Copyrighting the expression of new concepts is a tricky subject, because the idea is not copyrightable but the expression is. Chapter 8 goes into further detail on how one could make the distinction.

## Encryption and DMCAing an Interface

Patents and copyrights can be used to block interoperability, but neither is a 100 percent reliable, court-tested means of doing so. Congress invented a new type of law designed from the ground up to allow software authors to sue competitors who write interoperable programs. The reasoning behind the law is based on the protection of encryption.

### Bernstein v. U.S. Department of State

The ideal encryption scheme is one that takes coherent data and turns it into what seems like white noise but does so in such a way that the data can be perfectly extracted if looked at in exactly the right manner. As currently practiced, encryption is closely related to traditional math problems such as factoring numbers into primes and is in the same class of problems as the traveling salesman problem mentioned earlier. Encryption has been an important government tool for decades. During World War II, Alan Turing, the mathematician whose genius was mentioned in chapter 3, was instrumental in the United Kingdom's efforts to encrypt its communications and to decrypt those of the enemy; one could argue that the cracking of Germany's Enigma code was the key to winning the war in Europe. Turing's wartime work was an application of the imaginary tape computer he had described in 1936, but this time he used real electronic devices.[18]

Since then encryption has become increasingly important to civilians as well. Depending on the network, cell phone calls may be encrypted. When one makes an online purchase with a credit card (a process protected by patent 6,289,319), the card number is thankfully encrypted. On the other hand, encryption is as useful to terrorists and mobsters today as it was to the Nazis in the 1940s. U.S. export laws therefore regulate the dissemination of encryption devices of a certain strength.

Most software authors considered these laws to be just an annoyance. Programs such as Netscape needed to have a U.S.-only version with 128-bit encryption and an international version with weaker 64-bit encryption. Users would have to click an "I promise I'm in the U.S.A." button to get the fully functional version. Software on CDs would require either two printings or a cumbersome online upgrade for U.S. users. But for Daniel Bernstein, a graduate student in mathematics at the University of California at Berkeley whose work focused on encryption methods, it was more than a nuisance: under the letter of the law, he could not publish his papers, teach, or present his work at academic conferences.

In February 1995, Bernstein sued for clarification of the law. Subsequently, the court ruled that "the Export Administration Regulations, . . . insofar as they apply to or require licensing for encryption and decryption software and related devices and technology are in violation of the First Amendment."[19] Thanks to this ruling, the bureaucratic restrictions on encryption software have been weakened but not entirely removed. However, regulators have shifted their focus to the opposite end: decryption software.

---

18. Unfortunately, Turing was unable to further contribute to the development of computer science. His work was cut short in March 1952, when he was arrested for homosexual activity. Since sensitive government secrets could not be entrusted to a homosexual and the court-ordered estrogen treatment failed to cure him of the condition, he was fired from his position at government communication headquarters. He committed suicide in June 1954.

19. *Daniel Bernstein v. U.S. Department of State, et al.*, U.S. District Court, Northern District of California, No. C-95-0582 MHP 1996.

## *Motion Picture Association of America (MPAA) v. 2600 Magazine*

The Digital Millennium Copyright Act makes it illegal to distribute a device designed to circumvent a copy protection scheme, which is usually some method of encryption.[20] The intent is to prevent people from copying copyrighted materials such as movies or music. However, it is as easy to copy music or movies under the DMCA as before; companies actually use the law to sue authors of code when neither patents, copyrights, nor trade secrets would apply.

For example, movies on DVD are encrypted using the Content Scrambling Scheme (CSS), so when Jon Lech Johansen wrote the decryption component for a DVD player for Linux (deCSS), he violated the DMCA and thus committed a felony under U.S. law.[21] Most encryption depends on a key, which is an exceptionally long number that is kept secret. If I have the key, I can mash the message and the key together to produce gibberish to send to associates, and if they have the key, they can use it to restore the message to its original form. Most systems are much more complex, but the basic idea is the same: those with the key and some idea of how the scrambling works can read the message. Every DVD player has several CSS keys built in. Manufacturers must sign nondisclosure agreements with the Digital Versatile Disc Copy Control Association (DVD CCA) to the effect that they will keep these keys a closely guarded secret, and if they let the keys slip they will be liable for damages under traditional contract law.

But Johansen's group did not need to lift the keys from a DVD player. Every DVD movie in their living rooms contained a stream of encrypted information, and running the viewer on a laptop would yield the stream of unencrypted information. By comparing the two, the team could find clues to the key. Through such gathering of clues and computational brute force, the team successfully learned how CSS works. Of course, CSS was easy enough to crack because it had to comply with the still-extant U.S. export restrictions mandating a maximum strength to the encryption.[22]

20. 17 U.S.C. 1201(a)(2).

21. Jon is the most publicized member of the group but does not get credit for working out the CSS. In fact, three groups independently derived the system. For a history, see "CSS and deCSS" (www.lemuria.org/DeCSS/decss.html).

22. The preferred method circumvents the keys entirely. See Frank A. Stevenson, "Cryptanalysis of Contents Scrambling System," November 8, 1999 (www.lemuria.org/DeCSS/crypto.gq.nu/).

According to DVD CCA's frequently asked questions, "Despite legal 'trade secret' protection for CSS, the code for its algorithms and master keys—the main elements of its security—were stolen and posted on the Internet."[23] But trade secret protection applies only to parties who willingly enter into a contract containing a nondisclosure clause, and Johansen and his associates had never signed any such agreement with the DVD CCA. Despite the claims, no trade secret agreements had been violated.

The website continues, "Much like a copyrighted book cannot legally be scanned and posted on the Internet, protected software and encryption code cannot either." However, recall that independent authorship is a valid defense in copyright claims. The deCSS code was not scanned and posted but *derived* and posted, so Johansen's team violated no copyright laws either.

All of the traditional protections did not apply: the encryption method was too common to merit a patent; Johansen never agreed to keep the DVD CCA's trade secrets for it; he did not violate copyrights since he never saw the protected code and therefore could not have plagiarized. Fortunately for the DVD CCA, the DMCA provided a fourth type of IP protection with which it could prosecute those who disseminated the deCSS code.

The colorful world of phone phreaking—using and abusing the telephone grid for one's own amusement—has given rise to a publication called *2600 Magazine: The Hacker Quarterly*. Some of its readers perhaps committed felonies with the information therein, but most just enjoyed the ingenuity required to get around in a complex technical system. Either way, their magazine was protected by the First Amendment. The detective work behind the deCSS code fit right in to *2600*'s range of topics, so it published the code.

Although the code was now common knowledge, not much more could be done than before: to copy a DVD, one could make a verbatim copy of every last encrypted byte on the disk—no decryption required— and the new identical disk would work just as well. The difference was that DVDs could now be viewed (not just blindly copied) using software that had paid no fees to the DVD CCA. Furthermore, DVDs encrypted for the Asian or European region could be easily viewed in the United

23. DVD Copy Control Association, "Frequently Asked Questions" (www.dvdcca. org/faq.html).

States, and users could bypass the advertisements at the beginning of some DVDs. The MPAA sued *2600 Magazine,* basing its complaint in the DMCA.

The court, in its November 2001 ruling, acknowledged that code is both speech and a functional entity at once. "This reality obliges courts considering First Amendment claims in the context of the pending case to choose between two unattractive alternatives: either tolerate some impairment of communication in order to permit Congress to prohibit decryption that may lawfully be prevented, or tolerate some decryption in order to avoid some impairment of communication."[24] It chose to impair communication.

And so, when I wrote figure 7-1 into this manuscript and thus trafficked in a circumvention device, I infringed on the DVD CCA's newfound right to disallow the printing of anything equivalent to its decryption code. As a bonus, this is not only grounds for a civil suit but a felony under federal law, punishable by a $500,000 fine or five years in prison, or both.[25] Conversely, figure 7-2, describing how to build a small low-tech fertilizer bomb comparable to the large one used to destroy the Federal Building in Oklahoma City, is protected speech and may be printed without fear of prosecution.[26]

Encryption has come a long way. Initially a field in which mathematicians and computer scientists aggressively worked to out-technology each other, it has become flooded by an endless stream of legal battles—thanks to one act of Congress that outlawed improved encryption and another that outlawed decryption.

### Impact of the DMCA

Because IP protection on decryption programs has the broadest scope of all, the DMCA has had an impact on the interoperability of a wide

24. 273 F.3d 429 (2001).

25. Perhaps it is not a felony, since it takes one more item to do an actual decryption. The code here will decrypt a DVD title by title, whereas on a typical movie each chapter is a separate title. One still needs to derive the title key for each chapter before using this. For a program to derive the title keys, and many versions of the deCSS algorithm (including this one), see www.cs.cmu.edu/~dst/DeCSS/Gallery/.

26. The mess in Figure 7-1 may not seem to communicate anything at all but in its own way is a form of speech, stating an equation that transforms an integer into another integer. The courts agree that "free speech" means not only political speech but also arts and sciences. See, for example, *Miller* v. *California* (1973): "The First Amendment protects works which, taken as a whole, have serious literary, artistic, political, or scientific value." For one well versed in bit-shifting operations, figure 7-1 certainly has serious scientific value.

**Figure 7-1. The deCSS Code: Printing This Figure Is a Felony**

```
/* efdtt.c Author: Charles M. Hannum
   <root@ihack.net> */
/* Thanks to Phil Carmody <fatphil@asdf.org>
   for additional tweaks. */
/* Usage is: cat title-key scrambled.vob |
   efdtt >clear.vob */
#define m(i)(x[i]^s[i+84])<<
unsigned char x[5],y,s[2048]; main(n){
for(read(0,x,5); read(0,s,n=2048); write(1,s,n))
if(s[y=s[13]%8+20]/16%4==1){int i=m(1)17^256+
m(0)8,k=m(2)0,j=m(4)17^m(3)9^k*2-k%8^8,a=0,
c=26;for(s[y]-=16;--c;j*=2)a=a*2^i&1,
i=i/2^j&1<<24;for(j=127;++j<n ;c=c>y)
c+=y=i^i/8^i>>4^i>>12,i=i>>8^y<<17,a^=a>>14,
y=a^a*8^a<<6,a=a>>8^y<<9,k=s[j],
k="7Wo~'G_\216"[k&7]+2^"cr3sfw6v;*k+>/n."[k>>4]
*2^k*257/8,s[j]=k^(k&k*2&34)*6^c+~y;}}
```

variety of software. Once a company claims that it has a copy protection program, any other program that functions like it is in violation of the original program's DMCA protection. It is much the same as an over-broad patent, but without any of the hassle of filing for a patent and proving originality. On top of the immense breadth of protection granted

**Figure 7-2. How to Make a Fertilizer Bomb:**
**This Figure Is Protected by the First Amendment**

Fill a paper bag with fertilizer. Use fertilizer with high nitrogen content.

Top the bag with a layer of cotton.

Douse the cotton with diesel fuel.

Light the fuel; run as fast as you can.

the decryption program, Congress threw in felony charges as an added deterrent.

The claimed intent of the added protection is to prevent the copying of copyrighted music and movies, but the end result has been far removed from this original intent and is much closer to the potential misuses of patents discussed earlier, as a means of suing legitimate competitors out of the marketplace. In a similar manner, the DMCA has been bullying out of the market the producers of electronic book readers, printer cartridges, and even garage door openers.

The key provision of the DMCA is that no one may produce a device to circumvent a manufacturer's copy protection. The reader may still be unclear on what a copy protection scheme and a circumvention device are, but then so are the courts. The suits discussed next indicate that any attempt by Company A to make it difficult for Company B to make products that interoperate with A's is a copy-protection scheme. If B succeeds despite A's best efforts, then its product must be using a circumvention device, so A can sue under the DMCA.

The first of these suits was brought by Adobe, the steward of the Portable Document Format (PDF), which has a variant for electronic books. The eBook format has certain restrictions built in: users who open an eBook with Adobe Acrobat and click the print button will be warned that they are not allowed to print eBooks. Less ubiquitous document readers, such as ghostview, do not even understand the special eBook codes and will print the document like any other PDF.

Dmitri Sklyarov is a programmer for a Russian company that sells a program that can print eBooks. Adobe filed a complaint under the DMCA arguing that this was a circumvention of its copy protection. When Sklyarov attended a computer science conference in the United States, a team of federal agents greeted him with handcuffs and kept him in a U.S. prison for a month. Mathematicians and programmers, a normally apolitical bunch, were horrified.[27]

The next case involves Lexmark, which makes printers and their attendant printer cartridges, and Static Control, which makes printer cartridges that are compatible with Lexmark's printers. In order to be compatible, the cartridge must include a chip programmed with a short piece of code that can be used to verify whether the cartridge is authentic or

27. A year and a half after the arrest, a jury acquitted Sklyarov, finding that his violation of the DMCA was not "willful." See www.freesklyarov.org.

not. Making two pieces of hardware compatible now becomes a software issue. Lexmark claims that the code is a copy protection scheme, so if Static Control's cartridges work in Lexmark's printers, Static Control must have circumvented its copy protection. As of this writing, the District Court of the Eastern District of Kentucky ruled that Static Control is in violation of the DMCA and therefore must halt its production.[28] However, the District Court of the Sixth Circuit chose to use a narrow interpretation of the DMCA that excluded Lexmark's code.[29] As a result, Static Control was allowed to resume production. The Supreme Court chose not to hear this portion of the case, thus failing to reject the narrow interpretation.[30] The case continues in the district court.

Another DMCA complaint was filed by Chamberlain, maker of garage door openers and their attendant remote controls. Since one remote should not open every door on the block, users can set a key on their remote and on the opener itself so that only one garage door will respond to one remote. On top of this, Chamberlain garage door openers and remotes keep track of how often the button is pressed, and the opener sends that figure and the key to the garage door, which verifies that the information is correct. Notice the resemblance to encryption: the sender uses a key to transmit a signal that only a receiver with the same key will accept.[31]

Skylink makes replacement remote controls for all the poor souls who lost their original remote. Skylink's engineers learned which signals are sent by a Chamberlain remote and then made a control that imitates the same signals. Chamberlain sued, claiming its signals were a copy protection scheme that Skylink had circumvented, thereby violating the DMCA.

The CAFC ruled in summary judgment against Chamberlain.[32] But the case, on top of Dmitiri's story, Lexmark's suit, and other seeming abuses

28. No. 02-571-KSF (ED Kentucky, February 27, 2003).
29. No. 03-5400, 2004 U.S. Dist. (6th Cir. Oct. 26, 2004).
30. The Supreme Court has refused to hear Lexmark's request for a hearing to overturn the district court's ruling striking down the preliminary injunction, meaning that Static Control is free to produce allegedly infringing cartridges during the trial. However, the trial itself has not yet been held. See Ken Fisher, "Supreme Court Denies Lexmark's Hearing Request," *Ars Technica*, June 6, 2005, arstechnica.com/news.ars/post/20050606-4973.html.
31. The mechanism matches keyed encryption but is significantly weaker: the remote sends the key and then the number of button presses the remote control knows, without mashing the two together in any way. But ours is not to dictate when a claimed copy protection scheme is trivial or not.
32. *Chamberlain Group, Inc.* v. *Skylink Techs. Inc.*, No. 04-1118, 2004 WL 1932660 (Fed. Cir. Aug. 31, 2004).

of the DMCA, made it obvious that the letter of the DMCA law stifled competition and interoperability. As of this writing, revisions to the DMCA are in committee in Congress.[33]

If the DMCA is rewritten but not eliminated, one can expect this new and supremely broad form of IP protection to continue to cause problems for a more restricted but still potentially large set of software program-mers. If Microsoft claims that its Windows Media Audio (WMA) format includes an encryption scheme, then Microsoft will be the only company in the world with the right to sell programs that can read the WMA data structure. Compare this with the DOC format, which Microsoft has been trying to maintain exclusive control of for years: under the DMCA it could simply sue anyone who writes WMA-compatible audio players right now.

Some may think that the DMCA has a valid intent: DOC files are probably written by the file's owner, while WMA files are probably music written and copyrighted by someone else. However, there is no way to write a law that covers the WMA data structure but not the DOC struc-ture. Despite the intent of the format's authors, users will not necessarily fall in line with Microsoft's intended use of its formats: authors can pub-lish copyrighted novels in DOC format, and garage bands can give away their work in WMA format.

Furthermore, many data structures are merely containers. For exam-ple, the Binary Large Object (BLOB) records in a database could hold audio or text files, and some misguided uses of XML encode music, while XML is also used for Word's DOC format. Protecting the copyrighted works of artists is a valid goal, but doing it by outlawing certain uses of certain data structures is a fundamentally flawed means of doing so. As honest as its intent may have been, the DMCA has become a patent replacement with far-reaching impact on fields that have nothing to do with music or movies.

### Inefficacy of Code Restrictions

Another problem is that the DMCA is wholly ineffective in preventing the copying of any sort of data. The Internet battle cry of old was "Infor-mation wants to be free," and although many people interpreted this to mean "I don't want to pay for things online," it actually meant "restrict-ing information is an impossible task."

33. See the Digital Media Consumers' Rights Act of 2005, H.R. 1201, 109 Cong. (2005).

Linux users who wish to watch their DVDs on their computers must search for "xine D5D" and then download the code from Brazil. But the standard Linux DVD copying software (cdrecord) blindly copies bits from one disc to another, making absolutely no effort to decrypt the data it is copying and is therefore entirely legal.

In terms of preventing the copying of copyrighted works, there is absolutely nothing that a person cannot do under the DMCA that could have been done without it. However, as demonstrated earlier, this new IP protection has made it possible for businesses to harass competitors in court in situations where this was not possible using any other form of IP protection.

On the encryption side, when export restrictions were at their height, users who could not click the "I promise I'm in the U.S.A." button to download the strong-encryption version could download it from Australia. The sysadmins of terrorist organizations had to download code for 64-bit encryption and then change a handful of parameters to get 128-bit encryption. Or they could download it from Australia.

Simply put, once a person has published an algorithm, it is available to the whole world. It may be possible to effectively control enriched uranium, but controlling the dissemination of large prime numbers is a lost cause.

Restricting research in encryption or decryption is equally misguided. The first step in improving anything—physical or conceptual—is to understand its weaknesses. Making it illegal to search for loopholes in encryption and computer security basically makes it illegal to learn from existing schemes and guarantees that encryption techniques will never improve.

The DMCA allows the authors of certain types of software to declare themselves to be owners of a patent-like right to exclude, so the same cost-benefit analysis needs to be done for the DMCA as for patents: does the economic benefit to granting such a monopoly right outweigh the deadweight loss monopolists cause in the marketplace? Although I do not discuss the benefits of an appropriately narrow version of the DMCA here, the cost side of the equation is especially large, because an author may simply declare himself to be the owner of a copy protection scheme, just as copyright is paperwork-free, but as in the case of a patent, the author may sue independent inventors.

# CHAPTER EIGHT

# Protecting Text

Two of the most common and sensible solutions to the problems with software patents rest on the basic principle that protection should be granted for an implementation, not an idea. For a program, that means protecting the text of the source code.

The first, relatively moderate solution is to patent the source code instead of vague descriptions or flowcharts. The second is to eliminate software patents entirely and protect the text of software only by copyright. However, because copyright is designed around fields such as literature, the visual arts, and music, it needs some modification in order to apply to code.

Having resolved to protect only the implementation, how can it be separated from the idea it represents? The courts have a means, known as the abstraction-filtration-comparison test, which is famously vague and difficult to implement—but this does not mean that copyright is impossible to apply. By looking at both the final code and the process by which the code is written, the courts give themselves more ground to look for more clearly defined types of infringement.

Both patents on source code and copyright protect the text that implements the invention from imitation. The key difference between the two is that independent invention cannot be used as a defense against claims of patent infringement, meaning that a coincidental match between two patented algorithms would be grounds for a lawsuit. In a world where code is protected by copyright, there would be no grounds unless the second inventor had plagiarized the work of the first.

## The Social Contract and Filing Source Code

To entice people to divulge their innovations instead of keeping them a guarded secret, the government offers them 20 years of legal protection if they file a patent. In return, the world at large gets a detailed description of how the magic was done. Other inventors or scientists can learn from this information, even if they cannot directly profit from it. The ideal from an economic perspective would be that others learn from the patent and implement the ideas embodied therein in new and unique ways, which they may then patent. The resulting market would be filled with clearly differentiated implementations, and all could profit.

Before this can happen, the implementation of the algorithm needs to be made public. Currently, few software patents discuss implementation, and only a very small sample includes actual source code. This arrangement breaks the implicit social contract, since the interface is public to begin with, while the implementation remains hidden. In exchange for granting a 20-year monopoly, the public gets nothing.

For most patent applications, the law demands that precise details be disclosed: "The specification shall contain a written description of the invention, and of the manner and process of making and using it, in such full, clear, concise, and exact terms as to enable any person skilled in the art to which it pertains, or with which it is most nearly connected, to make and use the same."[1] This stipulation is very sensible: it would be prohibitively expensive for every inventor of a new tractor or airplane engine to deliver a working model to the U.S. Patent and Trademark Office (USPTO). Step-by-step manufacturing instructions are the next best thing. Because a patent must enable the reader to do something that could not be done without the document, this rule is known as the *enablement requirement*. For biotech patents, however, step-by-step instructions for creating a new life form are beyond human abilities, so the USPTO requires inventors in this field to deposit an actual sample in certain cases.[2]

In the case of computer-related inventions, the examination guide merely states: "An applicant's specification must reasonably convey to

1. 35 U.S.C. §112.
2. 37 C.F.R. §1.802.

those skilled in the art that the applicant was in possession of the claimed invention as of the date of invention."[3] No step-by-step manufacturing instructions are required, and the patent need not inform another person skilled in the art of computing anything about the implementation. What seems like a weaker standard for software stems from the fact that patents never need to declare obvious and trivial steps. In *Northern Telecom* v. *Datapoint*, one of the key cases asking what is adequate disclosure in a patent, the court concluded that the entire process of implementing a software concept is obvious to any programmer: "The conversion of a complete thought (as expressed in English and Mathematics . . .) into a language a machine understands is necessarily a mere clerical function to a skilled programmer."[4]

As legal scholar Dan Burk points out in his journal articles and testimony to the Federal Trade Commission (FTC), the Court of Appeals for the Federal Circuit (CAFC) has upheld this weaker standard for software.[5] "The Federal Circuit tells us that essentially there is no disclosure requirement for software. In cases that have come before that court where there has been a question about disclosing code or even a flowchart or some other indications of how software works, the Federal Circuit tells us that's not necessary."[6] "Tell us," he continues, "that it's a compiler; tell us that it's a spreadsheet. . . . You don't need to tell us what the code is. You don't need to give us a flowchart, don't need to give us any indication of how you do it, just tell us its function."[7]

Such low standards not only fail to uphold the social contract but do so in the area where it can best be upheld. Data storage and Internet bandwidth are cheap. If the USPTO can cover the expense of safely storing samples of genetic material and living organisms, it can certainly cover the expense of storing computer code.

### How to Obfuscate an Obvious Idea

The structure of software makes it very easy to write code quickly and relatively intuitively; the structure of a patent application makes it very easy to hide the fact that so little work was required. To turn three lines of code into a nonobvious and novel invention, describe it in language

3. USPTO Examination Guidelines for Computer-Related Inventions, sec. V, B(2).
4. 908 F.2d 931, 940–41, 15 USPQd 1321, 1328 (Fed. Cir. 1990).
5. Burk and Lemley (2002).
6. FTC (2002, p. 108).
7. FTC (2002, p. 134).

below the level at which a sane programmer would work. For example, to patent a procedure for doing a few arithmetical calculations using a programming language such as C or S, describe a set of registers that manipulate numbers represented in memory. To patent a form for entering numbers into a database, write a patent for a program to paint buttons and text boxes on a screen and then execute low-level functions to process the various operations users would perform. Of course, libraries abound that would allow such forms to be written with a few lines of code, but a patent claim mentioning just a handful of preexisting packages would have a slimmer chance of passing examination. Using this method, Brian Shuster turned the three lines of JavaScript code in figure 1-1 into 42 claims. At the extreme, nothing looks obvious in assembly language; similarly, nothing looks obvious when it is described in the meticulous step-by-step detail of typical claim language.

Of course, the same obfuscation could be achieved with source code: an applicant could send pages of C code instead of a few lines of JavaScript. It is the examiner's job to be sufficiently familiar with existing languages and function libraries to know that C is not the best mode for implementing pop-up windows.

At the other extreme, requiring source code forces applicants to pare overbroad claims down to the appropriate scale. Just as two designers who patent machines that do the same thing in substantially different ways are not infringing each other's patents, a claim on source code should not be a claim on any equivalent implementation that anyone ever dreams up. A patent for software on a general-purpose computer remains a patent on pure mathematical equations, but it can at least be a patent on a more limited range of equations.

Authors who claim a mathematical idea as their property should have to provide specific details about how their implementation differs from the theoretical algorithm—in the words of the *Gottschalk* v. *Benson* ruling (chapter 4), they would have to explain why it is not the case that "the patent would wholly pre-empt the mathematical formula and in practical effect would be a patent on the algorithm itself." Such a requirement can be satisfied only by a detailed specification of the algorithm and its implementation—source code.

### What Sort of Code Would Be Filed?

First, most of the code that goes into a program is simply not novel, being merely dull, boilerplate checks to make sure that memory is available, data are in the right format, and so forth. For retail software, a multitude of other considerations are also necessary but cannot be claimed as novel or nonobvious, such as support for foreign languages, an automated installation procedure, and animated characters. The actual implementation of an idea is clearest to the reader of the source code when all of these are omitted. As a further incentive against obfuscation and overgeneralization, it is in the interest of the patent applicant to implement code that is close to what competitors are expected to do: code at its least obfuscated will allow the most effective future claims.

The greatest embarrassment for a coder is to learn that a few pages of her best code could all have been done in a line or two. This carries over to formal patent procedure, via the *best-mode rule*: an inventor must file those techniques that he or she believes to be the best implementation of the invention.[8] Computer scientists exalt simplicity and clarity, so an application obfuscated with extraneous code or written at the wrong level may not be in compliance with the best-mode rule.

Claim language, though necessary, is not the most efficient means of describing software and therefore should be a descriptive supplement to the code itself. Applicants have every incentive to make hundreds of claims and leave it to the examiner to choose which are valid, but with code, such a verbose strategy may not be optimal.

### Source Code in the Public Domain

Because the description in code of a software invention is the invention itself, asking inventors to file source raises the possibility that users would download the program from the USPTO, saving the expense of purchasing it from the author. Since any patent (but a software patent) must describe the item with "such full, clear, concise, and exact terms as to enable any person skilled in the art . . . to make and use the same," this complaint is not new to software. A competent mechanic could download the patent for a tractor that satisfies the requirements and then build the tractor from scratch.

The considerations that keep people from seriously doing this are the same ones that would keep people from seriously downloading code from the USPTO web site and using it directly. Beyond having a good idea, a vendor adds value in the sense of knowing how to implement the idea in an efficient manner, how to have the invention interoperate with its sur-

8. This is explicitly applied to software in MPEP §2106, sec. V.

roundings, and what to do when things go wrong. All of this still holds for software: there is value to be added by the implementer on top of the bare-bones source code.

Recall that a good patent application would be one that is brief to the point of lacking the boilerplate memory-checking, error-handling, and animated characters. A user who insisted on downloading the software from the USPTO instead of purchasing a license would get code that clearly describes the implementation but that is somewhere between lacking bells and whistles and being entirely unusable in the real world. This is an ideal situation in that the inventor still has a market for the product, and others such as students and potential competitors can learn from the inventor. Both sides of the social contract are fulfilled.

However, if the software is so simple that a patent sketch embodies the entire innovation, such as a single function or data structure, then it is probably too close to pure mathematics to merit a patent. As for software authors who worry that it would be impossible to control the code even with the power afforded by a patent, they might want to keep the code a trade secret. The Coca-Cola Company has kept the details of its recipe a secret for a century, but since the life cycle of a version of a software release is only a few years, keeping the code a secret is not so Herculean a task. From the perspective of the social contract, inventors who do not want to entrust the public with details of their inventions have nothing to offer in exchange for the granting of a monopoly; the public has no obligations toward such persons.

### Why a Source Code Requirement May Not Work

The breadth of a patent could be narrower with source code than without, since some creative mathematician may be able to convince the court that another algorithm that achieves the same goal is sufficiently removed from the patented code. Filing source code with each patent application would thus provide a start to addressing the massive breadth of existing patents, which may solve some of the problems mentioned in chapter 5, where patent-holders with absurdly broad patents can run legally amok.

But whether the breadth of a patent is actually narrowed by listing more detail is not a settled question. The *doctrine of equivalents* states that a device that does not literally infringe a patent but that effectively implements the same device in the same manner is still infringing. Since all representations of a mathematical equation are equivalent, regardless of the language used or the details of coding, efforts to restrict the breadth of a software patent to only a few representations may be entirely futile, because judges may apply the doctrine of equivalents to state that any and all implementations of the patented algorithm continue to violate the patent. That is, the equivalence of all implementations of the same algorithm is a tough bundle to break up, and more precise wording of claims may not be sufficient to do so.

Nor would requiring source code address the problem of applying patents to a massively decentralized industry. The only way for coders to guarantee that their work is patent-free is to search the database of all existing patents in the software field and compare them with the work at hand. Even with all source code in plain text and indexed by the best search engines imaginable, this is still an absurdly onerous requirement to ask of all the coders in all the basements of the world's organizations.

## Copyrighting Code

Like a correctly implemented patent law, copyright law protects implementations instead of general algorithms and protects the source code from being parroted. It does so with much less paperwork and also resolves the absurdity of requiring constant patent searches by every coder in the world, because independent derivation would not constitute infringement. While patent-oriented intellectual property (IP) focuses on whether two programs seem to work in the same manner, copyright-oriented IP is concerned with whether one party plagiarized the work of another. Furthermore, any words put to paper or computer screen are automatically copyrighted, whereas patents must be explicitly applied for. So the easiest way to protect code from imitation is simply not to publish it; if the source code is leaked out, then the authors can fall back on copyright to halt further plagiarism.

### Trade Secrets and Reverse Engineering

The traditional method of keeping competitors from copying code is to keep it a secret. This is generally an effective strategy for code of reasonable complexity. As discussed in chapter 3, human-readable source code can be compiled into computer-readable object code. If a user were to print the object code, it would be gibberish. However, all is not lost: the user could run the program under a *debugger*.

A debugger runs the program step by step so that the programmer can search for errors in logic. The debugger executes a single line of code and displays it on the screen in more or less human-readable form.

Recall that a program may include a symbol table translating between human-readable and machine-readable forms, for example, between register `0x80aa4f8` and the variable `my_mothers_birthday`, or the command `print_date(my_mothers_birthday)` and the set of machine instructions that would make the computer do such a thing. Given a symbol table, the debugger could display these human-readable symbols while it runs the program, and the user could thus get a good idea of how the program works. But the programmer could easily strip the symbols from the code before making the program public. Then the debugger would have no idea of what `0x80aa4f8` means, and a user who ran the program under a debugger would have to read the raw assembly code.

This can be done for a short routine: the user can make careful notes about what low-level steps the computer is executing and get a good idea of what high-level code had caused these steps. But for anything longer than a few functions, the procedure is maddening. Disassemblers exist to automate the process, but they cannot recover certain pieces of data lost in compilation, such as variable names, macros, or comments. The broad overview of implementation may be discernible, but it was probably discernible from reading the manual; the more detailed questions about implementation are the most difficult ones to reverse-engineer. Code that has been run through any sort of optimization routines during compilation is especially difficult for humans to understand after decompilation— and there are even code obfuscators for the especially paranoid.

*Is Reverse Engineering Legal?* When a user downloads a program from some distant server, the server sends a copy to the closest router, which sends a copy to the next router, and so on down a long chain until it arrives at the user's computer, where a copy is saved on the hard drive. Then the program can be run, meaning that the computer makes a copy from the hard drive to memory, where some of the instructions will be copied to the processor.

A copyright-holder can expressly permit or deny any copying of his or her work. Because copying data is an inherent action of almost every step in a computing process, the copyright-holder can theoretically dictate exactly what the user may or may not do with the program.

Under the principle of *fair use*, however, copyright-holders may not restrict certain behaviors, such as including a passage from a novel in a critical analysis, presenting a low-resolution version of a drawing when discussing the work (see figure 2-1), or making a backup copy of a CD in case the original should become a coaster. U.S. copyright law also classifies as fair use any copying as a transient step in using a program for its intended purpose.

But loading the program into the debugger for reverse engineering is also a copying process, as is displaying the symbol table or printing lines of assembly code to the screen. In almost all cases, this is not the author's intended use of the program. Because the primary uses of reverse engineering (creating interoperable products and learning) are activities that benefit users, U.S. courts have favored its legality: as explained in the ruling in *Sega Enterprises, Ltd. v. Accolade, Inc.*: "Disassembly is a fair use of the copyrighted work, as a matter of law."[9] The primary exception is, of course, when the subject of the reverse engineering is a copy protection scheme, in which case the DMCA states that the reverse engineering is no longer fair use but a felony. Courts in other jurisdictions have drawn different rules: those in the European Union, for example, consider it illegal to reverse-engineer a program if the intent is to create a competing product.[10]

If a coding team should disassemble a competitor's product and then implement its own version, however, the original manufacturer could readily accuse it of cutting and pasting low-level code and thus violating a copyright. The typical solution is for one team to do the disassembly and write a high-level flowchart of the lessons learned, and then for another team, cordoned into a *clean room*, to write new code using only the flowchart. Since the group in the clean room can document that it never saw the original code, it cannot be accused of copyright infringement.

A final twist to the reverse-engineering question is the end-user license agreement (EULA). The EULA is the several pages of legal fine print that wraps a software CD, or the text users must sift through in their web browsers before being able to download the software. It typically includes a statement that the user may not reverse-engineer the program about to be used. The CAFC ruled in *Bowers v. Baystate Technologies* that such a license is valid, in the sense that it is not preempted by the general default right to reverse-engineer.[11] In a similar manner, employees of a company

9. 977 F.2d 1510 (9th Cir. 1992).
10. Cifuentes and Fitzgerald (1999).
11. 320 F.3d 1317 (CAFC 2003). Controlling software via EULA requires eternal vigilance because if a competitor should ever have means of obtaining the code without first

typically sign an agreement that they will not use code written on the job in other locations. Companies with a proprietary code base can therefore keep even the ideas and concepts from plagiarism by setting aside copyright law and resorting to a direct contract with users.

***Is Reverse Engineering Worth It?*** Suppose that a competitor wants to produce a knockoff program as quickly as possible. To this end, the competitor plans to reverse-engineer the original program and copy the low-level implementation into the knockoff. Even with a complete symbol table, this is no way to produce one's own working, bug-free code, because the existing code needs to be understood and fit into the copier's existing code base.

Programmers generally agree that the most painful activity imaginable is to read someone else's code. Personally, I have found that other coders always come up with exotic methods and structures that are not nearly as obvious in function as the exotic methods and structures I use in my own work and never place the explicatory comments where I need them. The cognitive effort required to understand someone else's writing and make it work seamlessly with my own is often more than required to just program from scratch. The task is even harder if I cannot ignore the implementation and use the interface alone but am forced to go into the functions and structures themselves to make the necessary tweaks.

Programming teams overcome problems with reading each other's code by copiously documenting every function (needless to say, there are programs to autogenerate documentation, such as doxygen), and by lecturing each other about the need to put more comments in the code itself. An outsider would have no access to the external documentation and would have access to the comments in the source code itself only at the discretion of the authors (who can easily strip them from any public versions of the source or object code). Recall Ronald Mann's interviews with venture capitalists regarding IP; they, too, felt that even if reverse engineering were easy, these practical considerations would make it a terrible way to write code:

Indeed, a number of my interview subjects . . . argued that [code protection] efforts are wasteful, because access to the actual code is

---

signing on to the terms of an EULA, then the default right of reverse engineering remains. For example, in *Atari Games Corp.* v. *Nintendo of America, Inc.* (975 F.2d 832, 24 USPQ 1015 [Fed. Cir. 1992]), Atari obtained Nintendo's code from Nintendo's copyright registration with the Library of Congress.

not useful for most types of reverse engineering. Those executives argued that the need to integrate the reverse-engineered software into the operating environment of the competitor would make it counterproductive to start from the code of the originating innovator. It normally would be easier, they say, to start from scratch writing code to implement the observed functionality, than it would be to start from the existing code and alter that code to match the reverse engineer's existing environment. From that perspective, the emphasis on the code that is at the foundation of the copyright protection renders it entirely irrelevant to the protection of the startup firm's work in progress.[12]

So why enforce copyrights on source code when that code can be effectively kept secret, and even if it is not, it would be "counterproductive" for competitors to use? Copyright protection guards against the sort of shady dealing all businesses wish to avoid: disgruntled employees copying the code and reusing it at the next firm that hires them, partners in a limited enterprise reusing code in other off-contract projects, or counterfeiters with CD burners mass-producing identical copies. The only behavior it would not address would be independent derivation by competitors.

### The Breadth of Copyright Protection

As with patents, the key economic question for copyright is how broad the protection should be. Protection in both cases should be broad enough to ensure that the original author will invest in creative work but should not be so broad as to stifle further innovation.

In the case of copyright, the focus is not whether two pieces of code function in the same manner but whether one is a plagiarism of the other. This can be difficult to determine, since code is much more terse than prose and is constrained by many standards.

Say that a company produces software for the administration of dental software and a hacker at a dental lab writes a new administration program by copying the screen layouts and workflow of the original software. Would there be grounds for copyright infringement? According to the broad interpretation of "expression of an idea," the imitator would likely be infringing. The imitator had likely seen the original program in

12. Mann (2004, p. 24).

operation, and even the most distant imitation would bear more similarity than Garbage Pail Kids do to Cabbage Patch Kids. This situation is fairly typical of any two programs that share a similar interface.[13]

If copyright is interpreted this broadly, it becomes equivalent to a patent on an interface, and, as discussed in chapter 2, such breadth is economically detrimental. However, such broad copyright would differ from a comparably broad patent in two ways. First, as already mentioned, independent invention is a defense against claims of copyright infringement, but this is not likely to help much for a public interface, since a defendant would have to prove that he or she had never seen the competitor's product. Second, a copyright lasts not twenty years, but the better part of a century.[14] By the time the copyright on a work of software expired, computers would look nothing like they do today.

To broadly interpret copyright on code is to allow copyright on the code's function. As chapters 5 and 7 showed, such property rights are too broad, and §102 of the Copyright Act expressly forbids copyright on the concept behind the code. Because it is the functional embodiment of mathematical ideas, copyright needs to be interpreted more narrowly for software than for cartoons.

The other option is to interpret copyright strictly—that is, to bar only plagiarism, whereby one coder looks at another coder's work and, rather than independently writing code to function in a similar manner, directly copies the code. The correct breadth recalls the rule of thumb that protecting the interface is detrimental but protecting the implementation from theft is essential, but using that rule in the copyright realm requires new considerations: copyright can be interpreted too narrowly, since a program with the variable names changed is still the same program.

13. This is not a hypothetical situation. In *Whelan v. Jaslow*, 797 F.2d 1222, 230 USPQ 481 (1986), the Supreme Court ruled that copyright applies to the broad structures of two programs; this part of the ruling has since been limited (some would say reversed) via the abstraction-filtration-comparison test discussed in the next section. The ruling also relied on the fact that the author of the imitating program, Rand Jaslow, was an associate of Whelan Associates and had access to the source code of the original program. Therefore there was a good likelihood that Jaslow had made a line-by-line copy and translation of the original. Using the process-oriented method discussed in the next section, Jaslow would likely have been found to be infringing without resort to any "look and feel" similarities.

14. For a human author, copyright lasts seventy years after his or her death; for a corporate author, ninety-five years from publication.

### Copyrighting the Implementation

If someone cuts and pastes code from one program into another without permission, it is an undisputed violation of copyright. Identifying the violation in practice is another matter. First, two pieces of code that are identical may not be copies of each other; and second, one piece of code that looks nothing like another may actually be a plagiarism.

***Can a Single Line of Code Be Copyrighted?*** Suppose that a homework assignment in a creative writing class is to "describe visiting Mr. Usher on a cloudy day," and a student hands in the following sentence: "During the whole of a dull, dark, and soundless day in the autumn of the year, when the clouds hung oppressively low in the heavens, I had been passing alone, on horseback, through a singularly dreary tract of country, and at length found myself, as the shades of evening drew on, within view of the melancholy House of Usher." There would be absolutely no doubt that the student had copied the opening of Edgar Allan Poe's "Fall of the House of Usher." The probability that some clever individual would independently write this sentence, without ever having read Poe, is simply nil.

Copyright provides exactly the right protection: the original author is protected from people who effortlessly copy the author's work. At the same time, other authors are in no way stifled, because there is no chance that they will accidentally write a near-verbatim version of "Fall of the House of Usher."

In contrast, code can easily be written independently. Suppose that a homework assignment in a computer science class is to "write a function to find a person with a given name in a linked list." It would be no surprise at all if a student handed in a function that matched the `find_person` function in figure 3-3 down to the punctuation.

The Santa Cruz Operation (SCO) and International Business Machines (IBM) have spent a few million dollars in legal fees battling over IBM's alleged infringement of SCO's copyright on UNIX's source code. Written by Dennis Ritchie and Brian Kernighan at Bell Labs in the 1970s, UNIX's source code followed a long path: AT&T initially owned UNIX, but eventually spun off the UNIX development group as UNIX Systems Lab (USL), which sold UNIX's rights to Novell, which granted rights to SCO, which contracted the code to IBM. IBM eventually changed its mind about working with SCO and decided to put its efforts into Linux. Playing the part of the spurned goods vendor abandoned by the labor-oriented side of the market, SCO sued IBM, claiming that IBM had cut and pasted code from UNIX into Linux.

In the court papers, SCO listed a series of file names common to both UNIX and Linux, charging that "persons as yet unknown copied these files into Linux, erasing the USL copyright attribution in the process."[15] Two such files with the same name, *signal.h,* do indeed share some lines of code. Here is a sample of the first six signals:

```
#define SIGHUP 1
#define SIGINT 2
#define SIGQUIT 3
#define SIGILL 4
#define SIGTRAP 5
#define SIGABRT 6
```

Are there lines in the UNIX version of *signal.h* that exactly match? Absolutely—in fact, this is just a sample of the verbatim matches. But line-by-line implementation is not the level at which two works should be compared.

Both files have these lines in compliance with an Institute of Electrical and Electronics Engineers (IEEE) standard named POSIX (Portable Operating System Interface). UNIX, Linux, and a dozen other operating systems ending in the letter X all follow that standard—which specifies that SIGHUP must equal one, SIGINT must equal two, and so on. The standard is open, in the sense that anyone may implement it. However, SCO's claim is not about conceptual similarities between UNIX and Linux but about plagiarism, in which someone had cut and pasted from UNIX's source code, "erasing the USL copyright attribution in the process."

C coding standards provide only two ways to define the constant SIGQUIT as three, and this is the more sensible of the two. If 100 undergraduates were instructed to "write a header to define the first six signals in the POSIX standard," about 90 of their papers would match the code verbatim, and the remaining would lose points. The fact that six lines match says nothing about whether the author of the Linux version (Linus

---

15. Plaintiff's Revised Supplemental Response to Defendant's First and Second Set of Interrogatories, section "Supplemental Response to Interrogatory no. 12," reprinted at www.groklaw.net/article.php?story=20040215015800694.

Torvalds) had seen and copied the AT&T UNIX version. In fact, Warren Toomey of the UNIX Heritage Society did a painfully detailed analysis of the minor differences in the early versions of *signal.h* and gave a great deal of evidence that Linus did not crib from AT&T.[16]

***The Opinion of the Courts.*** The copyright equivalent to a patent's obvious inventions is the *scène à faire,* which the legal literature translates as "a scene that must be done." For example, in a movie in which the hero must defuse a bomb, the bomb absolutely must have a clock attached, and the hero must then defuse the bomb with mere seconds to spare. Characters, locations, and circumstances may vary, but the nick-of-time format is constant and requisite for this genre of film. Therefore the maker of one bomb-defusing action movie cannot sue a competitor for copyright infringement just because the other movie also had a bomb with a clock attached that was defused just in time.

In the POSIX standard, `SIGQUIT` must be three; in C, the only reasonable way to implement this is via the preprocessor directive above. The preceding code is thus a perfect example of a *scène à faire.* A more elaborate example is provided by *Lexmark International* v. *Static Control Components.* Recall that Lexmark's printer cartridges had a short program, 55 characters long, which Static Control copied verbatim onto its cartridges. Beyond claims under the Digital Millennium Copyright Act (DMCA), Lexmark charged that Static Control had violated the copyright on Lexmark's little program. The circuit court ruled that the code is a *scène à faire*: since there is no way to comply with the standard implicitly established by the printer except by the verbatim repetition of Lexmark's code, Static Control was not guilty of copyright infringement for making such a copy.

As discussed in chapter 7, it would be economically detrimental to allow the copyright of languages. The *scène à faire* rule indicates that a copyright on a language would not pass legal muster either: if the only way to interoperate with a program is via a sequence of magic words, those words may become a *scène à faire* no matter how much creativity originally went into authoring those words.

Admittedly, the line between a *scène à faire* and a creative work is blurred. POSIX implementations are like love poems: all express approximately the same idea, although some do so in an innovative manner. The

---

16. Warren Toomey, "Signal.h," *Groklaw,* March 1, 2004 (www.groklaw.net/article. php?story=2004022923000172).

problem for authors of software is that conceptual similarity opens the door to unnecessary litigation and harassment over claims of plagiarism.

*Porting and Translating.* There are three types of derivative work in the programming world. The first is functional work that interoperates with the original, such as a specialized spreadsheet for Microsoft Excel. As mentioned in chapter 7 and as indicated by the *scène à faire* rule, copyrights should not apply to the standards necessary for communication between interoperating programs.

The other two derivative types are porting and translating. Porting consists of taking code written for one set of libraries (such as those for Windows) and modifying it to work with another set (such as those for MacOS). Translating consists of taking code written in one language (such as C) and rewriting it in another (such as FORTRAN). Both of these types are tedious, frustrating, and basically mechanical processes.

In FORTRAN, the definition for SIGQUIT would look like this:

```
integer SIGQUIT
parameter (SIGQUIT = 3).
```

But if a FORTRAN programmer had looked at AT&T code and translated it to FORTRAN, he or she would be plagiarizing the code. That is, it is possible to interpret copyright too narrowly: a good copyright law should cover not simply the specific letters an author has written down but also undue imitation even after basic translations or modifications.

*Can a Single Function Be Copyrighted?* Copyright law as it stands today has much greater respect for the idea of a mathematical exception than current patent law. Recall from page 117 that the list of allowable subjects for copyright in 17 U.S. Code §102 is followed by an equally long listing of the subjects to which copyright may not apply, including "any idea, procedure, process, system, method of operation, concept, principle, or discovery." Conversely, Jefferson's patent law has no such pessimistic list of exclusions. Instead, one must look to judicial interpretation to find the statement of the mathematical exception. Such judicial support is easy to find; to give yet another example, the ruling in *Mackay Radio & Telegraph Co. v. Radio Corp. of America* stated that "a scientific truth, or the mathematical expression of it, is not a patentable invention."[17]

Because the mathematical exception is so clearly codified in copyright law, while the scientific and mathematical exceptions to patents are a

17. 306 U.S. 86, 94 (1939).

matter of common law, much more care is taken to exclude ideas and facts from copyright than from patents. Feist Publications basically copied the telephone listings compiled by Rural Telephone Service verbatim, but because telephone numbers are facts and not an original work, the Supreme Court ruled that Feist had done no wrong.[18] Meredith Corporation published a book of yogurt recipes that matched the recipes in a Publications International recipe book, although the order and presentation differed in details such as the "pictorial representations of the final products upon which the yogurt devotee may longingly fixate."[19] The court found no copyright infringement. "Although the inventions of 'Swiss 'n' Cheddar Cheeseballs' and 'Mediterranean Meatball Salad' were at some time original, there can be no monopoly in the copyright sense in the ideas for producing certain foodstuffs." Publications International could copyright "only the manner and order in which [the recipes] are presented."

Applied to software, the culmination of such rulings is the abstraction-filtration-comparison (AFC) test, first proposed in *Computer Associates International v. Altai.*[20] A court that hopes to determine whether a program is infringing the copyright of another must first abstract out the root algorithm the program expresses, then filter that algorithm from both programs, and then compare the remaining bits of expression. This would be comparable to replacing all of the yogurt recipes with markers, leaving only their order and accompanying photos.

The AFC test is difficult (some argue, impossible) for a court to apply objectively. However, the ideal law is one that never sees a courtroom because parties know exactly how to comply, and in this respect the AFC test may work rather well. A new program that included a nontrivial amount of code cut and pasted from a competitor's would clearly fail to pass the AFC test, while an imitator who learned from a competitor's code and then wrote new code based upon the lessons learned therefrom could easily ensure that the resulting code would pass AFC muster.

What if an imitator copied the original code and then made incremental and irrelevant modifications, such as renaming variables or shuffling the order of the functions? Then, at some point in development, the

18. *Feist Publications v. Rural Telephone Corp.*, 499 U.S. 340 (1991).
19. *Publications International, Ltd. v. Meredith Corporation*, 88 F.3d 473 (7th Cir. 1996).
20. 982 F.2d 693, 23 USPQ2d 1241 (2d Cir. 1992).

copier would have still cut and pasted the code and violated copyright, even if the final product looked dissimilar to the original. Conversely, if a competitor can produce a series of incremental steps toward a program that will in the end be dissimilar to the program the competitor is copying, then the competitor has just gone through a process much closer to the legal act of rederivation than to illegal plagiarism.

In short, the process matters, and it may give a clearer approach to determining infringement than the AFC test. Every algebra textbook on high school shelves today includes the quadratic equation, the algorithm for completing the square, and a dozen other standard ideas and facts. If the author of a new textbook were to open an existing text and begin copying, such behavior would be considered plagiarism, even if the new author should switch variable names or make other modifications. If the new author read one or many existing texts, took notes on their content, and began writing, effectively rederiving high school algebra anew, the resulting book would be an original work. The author may have depended on notes cribbed from others, but the derivation is his. For a textbook, there may or may not be evidence of the process of authorship. But the process is transparent for the typical program, even after the fact.

*Version Control.* Few if any programs spring whole from the programmer's mind. If they do, they are probably too trivial to fall within the scope of a good copy-protection law. Instead, programmers start with a simple skeleton, and perhaps notes written in complete sentences, and then build up new features with each step. Unlike the romantic playwright who burns his old manuscripts to keep warm, coders care deeply about keeping good records—and the law can take advantage of that.

Since programmers do nothing better than write programs to facilitate programming, there are dozens of recordkeeping systems, such as the concurrent versioning system (CVS) and its successor, subversion. As both names indicate, the programs focus on managing the dozens of versions and subversions of any single program. These systems have their flaws, so some users prefer Aegis, Arch, BitKeeper, Codeville, ClearCase, Katie, Monotone, Perforce, Razor, Stellation, or Vesta—some software companies have even written their own in-house version control from scratch. At the very least, any good programmer keeps backup copies of his or her work. A programmer—or a lawyer—may easily query these systems for a copy of the program as it looked six months or a year ago.[21] Under a good copyright regime, programmers would want to keep full records of past versions of the program. Fortunately, this requirement comports with good programming style and usual custom, so is no more onerous than the habits a good programmer has to begin with.

Given all of this information, it should be easy to determine whether a new program is parroting an old one or has evolved naturally. It is the process that determines whether the new author is plagiarizing or rederiving, and the process of coding is clearly recorded and archived. Could someone fake the records after the fact? Yes, but the task would entail more than just developing the program. One would have to rewrite a skeleton that bore distant similarity to the copyrighted work and then invent steps by which it would evolve into the final state. In other words, the copyrighted work would save a potential copier neither time nor effort.

The difficult-to-apply abstraction-filtration-comparison test can be substantially replaced by the simpler criterion of whether new authors developed their code base by copying and pasting it from elsewhere or by rederiving it. Focusing on the process brings in a wealth of new information, and an arbitrator can search for a smoking gun of plagiarism throughout the project. If parts were directly copied at any point, this would likely be sufficient to find infringement even after the AFC test (at least at the point in the revision history that the copy was made); if no parts were directly copied, there would likely be no similarity after one applied abstraction and filtration.

Is searching for direct plagiarism throughout the version history identical to applying the AFC test to the end product? They differ in one star case, *Computer Associates* v. *Altai*, which introduced the AFC test itself. The court applied the test to the two parties' final products and found sufficient differences to proclaim no infringement. However, one designer of Altai's program, who had once worked for Computer Associates (CA), had used CA source code in Altai's program; during the trial it was found that 30 percent of an earlier draft of Altai's program was copied directly from CA. The court applied its new AFC test to the final version of Altai's program and found no infringement, but if it had applied the test to the

21. Of course, slips still happen. In the copyright-infringement case of *Compuware* v. *IBM*, IBM was unable to produce early versions of the code Compuware claimed IBM had stolen until the last minute—when the code was found in a closet in Sydney, Australia. Nick Bunkley, "IBM Must Pay Compuware," *Detroit News*, September 28, 2004 (www.detnews.com/2004/technology/0409/29/b01-286633.htm).

earlier draft, it is almost certain that it would have found some expressive elements copied.[22] Applying the AFC test to every step of a program's cretion clearly provides more opportunities to find infringement, but in cases where it is present, applying the test is significantly easier.

The economically ideal law allows competition by diligent competitors but does not allow blind imitation. Everything an arbitrator needs to distinguish the diligent from the lazy exists in the records.

22. Some fear that even substantial direct plagiarism may still not count as infringement after abstraction and filtration. There is little if any evidence that the courts have interpreted or would interpret the AFC so zealously. But if they did, we could borrow a new type of intellectual property protection from database authors, who have had no protection since *Feist*. Often referred to as "sweat of the brow protection," it matches copyright in that it bars plagiarism and derivative works in a similar manner; its sole difference is that it does not demand that the work involve creativity. Sweat of the brow protection for databases exists in the EU; as of this writing, attempts to establish it in the United States have failed. Applying such protection to software would moot the AFC test, but it would create its own problems in determining when two programs or databases match because they document the same concepts or facts and when they match because of plagiarism. That is, the AFC test applied to the entire version history and sweat of the brow protection would ask an identical question: was there substantial plagiarism at some point in the version history?

# CHAPTER NINE

# Policy Recommendations

The Federal Trade Commission (FTC) is in the business of preventing overbroad monopolies. Of late, the U.S. Patent and Trademark Office (USPTO) has been granting overbroad monopolies. In October 2003, in the spirit of its mandate, the FTC published a report stating recommendations to reform the patent system.[1] Here are two that reflect the FTC's desire to have the patent system focus more on maximizing total economic benefit:

> *Recommendation 6:* Consider possible harm to competition—along with other possible benefits and costs—before extending the scope of patentable subject matter.
>
> *Recommendation 10:* Expand consideration of economic learning and competition policy concerns in patent law decision making.

These recommendations were actually somewhat contentious. In reply to the FTC's report, the Intellectual Property Owners Association (IPO) commented:

1. FTC (2003).

IPO does not . . . believe that the courts or USPTO should actively attempt to balance patent law with economic policy through strategies such as limiting the scope of patentable subject matter or denying the grant or limiting enforcement of a patent. IPO believes that such an attempt would profoundly undercut the foundation of the patent system. . . . The greater good is best served when the courts and USPTO grant and enforce patents without consideration to the net economic good or net economic harm caused by a single patent.[2]

IPO's statement acknowledges that a balance could be struck where limits on patents could be informed by economic policy. At the same time, it says that the economic good of individual patents should not be a consideration for approval. I agree: guessing at such microlevel economic effects is a crapshoot.[3] But one *can* make valid predictions about the overall benefit or loss on the basis of large genres of patents, as the FTC recommends.

Not only do I (and the FTC) agree that we should make such evaluations, but some argue that it is Congress's obligation to do so, as indicated in Article I, section 8, clause 8 of the U.S. Constitution: "The Congress shall have power to . . . promote the progress of science and useful arts, by securing for limited times to authors and inventors the exclusive right to their respective writings and discoveries." According to Lawrence Lessig, Stanford and University of Chicago law professor, this clause "sets forth the precise reason for the power—to promote the progress of science and useful arts. It is for those reasons, and those reasons only, that Congress may grant an exclusive right—otherwise known as a monopoly."[4] Not only does it make sense for patent law to be in harmony with economic reality, but, as Lessig emphasizes, it is Congress's *obligation* to ensure that patent law promotes rather than hinders progress, and to the extent that patent law does not promote progress, it is unconstitutional. It is in this context that this book was written, and on which this chapter focuses.

2. Press release, July 8, 2004, replying to the FTC report discussed in this chapter. IPO's release is available in its archive of legislative and international issues position statements at http://www.ipo.org/.
3. For some good reasons why this is so, see FTC (2003, chap. 4, p. 7), which concurs with IPO that individual patents should not be conditional on a full economic cost-benefit analysis.
4. Lessig (1999, p. 133).

## An Act of Congress

Although Congress is supposed to allow patent protection only under certain conditions, it has been somewhat lax in this regard when it comes to software patents. By leaving the law governing what may be patented as a single sentence, it has left the decision of what is or is not patentable to a long string of judges and hundreds of individual patent officers. But it is not the judge's job to ask whether software should be patentable, only whether software fits the vague definition of patentable subject matter codified by Congress. Nor is it the job of the patent officers, who simply try their best to conform to the ever-changing opinions of the court.

Thus this book's primary policy recommendation is that Congress actually consider and debate whether software is indeed patentable subject matter. Because there is a bright line between a state machine and the states to which it has been set, physical inventions and software can easily follow different laws.

Some would argue that to consider each industry or technology separately would open a can of worms since every industry would then battle for stronger or weaker protections. The fact is, these battles are already being fought in the courts, which is an inappropriate venue for such debate. Moreover, some precedent has been set for having different patent laws for different types of invention: the U.S. Code already contains specific rules about the patenting of genetic material.

It would be counterproductive to have different laws covering different physical fields because of the ease of reclassifying a patent from one category to another. Different laws would simply induce reshuffling and reclassification instead of real change. But software has no physical manifestation except in the state of a state machine. If the physical state machine is patentable and the state is not, there would be no loss of clarity, and no way to shuffle code into physical machines (except via further innovation in the design of new machines).

A moderate but complex alternative would be to continue to allow software patents, but to make significant changes to the existing rules. A much simpler and potentially more effective suggestion would be to stop providing patent protection to software altogether, and instead provide much more limited facilities to ensure that copyright is appropriately applied.

## Restricted Patent Regimes

If software patents are to remain in use, major reforms must be made in how those patents are evaluated. Although it is easy to confuse the two, *it is the implementation, not the idea, that is patentable.*[5]

The structure of software, as discussed in chapter 3, is such that any large problem can be broken down by a competent practitioner into smaller problems that can be surmounted and then aggregated to solve the larger problem—meaning that, given the idea, the implementation approaches obviousness. Any small problem that is not obvious is likely to be a purely mathematical algorithm (in the style of *Gottschalk* v. *Benson*)—which is not patentable either.

There may be a narrow class of programs for which the implementation itself is neither obvious nor an innovative mathematical algorithm. If such a class exists, then it alone deserves patent protection. Here are some suggestions for how to find this class of patents, help block or invalidate patents outside this class, and provide the appropriate breadth of protection for those within it.

### Enforce Nonobviousness

The USPTO's corporate plan used to state that "the Patent Business is one of the PTO's three core businesses. The primary mission of the Patent Business is to help customers get patents."[6] The goal should not be to help customers get patents, however, but to evaluate which patents are worth granting. It may be better to turn away a marginal patent than allow it to haunt the legal system for 20 years. Furthermore, the review process depends too heavily on prior patent filings and not enough on the experience of programmers in the field. Many complain that such a process sometimes causes plain old common sense to disappear.

As discussed in chapter 5, it has been estimated that 58 percent of software patent applications cite no nonpatent prior art. Indeed, many if not most ideas in the journals and hard drives of practitioners appear nowhere in the USPTO's archives. Yet to omit such details is to deny the

5. I am in complete agreement with the courts on this. See the ruling in *Diamond* v. *Diehr* in chapter 4, or the decision regarding *Rubber-Tip Pencil Co.* v. *Howard* (87 US 498, 1874): "An idea of itself is not patentable."
6. USPTO FY2001 Corporate Plan, at www.uspto.gov/web/offices/com/corpplan/pt04.pdf. This language has since been deleted from the corporate plan owing to embarrassing press.

reality of the software industry. Any patent application that fails to acknowledge the world outside the USPTO's doorstep should be rejected.

In the words of a National Research Council (NRC) report: "The requirement that to qualify for a patent an invention cannot be obvious to a person of ordinary skill in the art should be assiduously observed. In an area . . . where the common general knowledge is not fully described in published literature that is likely to be consulted by patent examiners, another method of determining the state of general knowledge needs to be employed."[7] The NRC recommends an open post-grant review process to help bring in the necessary information.

### Simplify the Process of Overturning Patents

The restrictions on post-grant review need to be significantly reduced. In line with NRC's report, recommendation 1 of the FTC's report suggests that legislation should be enacted "to create a new administrative procedure to allow post-grant review of and opposition to patents." Without such a system in place, the only way to dispute a patent is through the legal system, which is the most expensive and inefficient option that one could imagine.

Again, it may be worth having separate rules for reevaluating software and physical patents, since a preponderance of patents in the software field are neither obvious nor novel. Patents cannot be disputed on the basis of breadth or subject matter: if in the words of the *Gottschalk* v. *Benson* ruling, a "patent would wholly pre-empt the mathematical formula and in practical effect would be a patent on the algorithm itself," there would be grounds for overturning the patent—yet there currently exists no administrative procedure to do so.

### Extension versus Application

Mathematical equations rewritten with real-world variable names should not be patentable. This is what Thomas Jefferson seems to have believed, and what the Supreme Court seems to have decided in its trilogy of rulings. But the ruling has been entirely forgotten in favor of the *In re Alappat* and *State Street* conclusions, which broadly apply patents to "anything made by man under the sun." The courts should be much more careful in making sure that patent applicants seek to protect an invention that incorporates the math into a larger physically innovative device, thus substantially extending the math beyond a direct application. Patent

7. Merrill, Levin, and Meyers (2004, p. 81).

applications whose sole novelty is in the assignment of real-world names to variables should not be granted. Applicants typically make every effort to imply a novel extension into the physical world in the wording of their patents. Examiners do not need to exclude any claims that seem to be on the borderline between having an inventive physical step or not, but may simply add a caveat to the claims that they do not apply when implemented via a program on an uninventive general-purpose computer.

### Interface versus Implementation

Patents should be about the engineering of machines, not about concepts. It is the money, time, and work that went into the design of the machine that may not be economically feasible on the unprotected free market. It only takes a single squashed banana to conceive of a banana protective device, but to select the right materials, design the correct shape, and test and revise and retest the prototypes takes much longer. This distinction between idea and engineering has been forgotten in the case of code, where the detailed description of an idea and the implementation of an idea are the same thing. As Brian Kahin explains, "To design it is to build it."[8] The distinction needs to be rediscovered: the code should be patented, not the idea.

If the idea itself were patented, then the first to invent it could claim a monopoly on an entire market, and no one could produce a program that could compete with the monopolist. This is far too broad a monopoly compared with what would be required to entice a company to hire creative programmers. Thanks to the rule that implementations and not ideas are patented, the markets for physical goods are filled with products that are distinct and competitive; the same should hold for software.

### File the Source Code

Prozac was not patented on a claim along the lines of "I have come up with a chemical that alleviates depression"—it was a complete description of the molecule itself that was patented. Meanwhile, programs are patented on the claim that the applicant is in possession of a program that does certain things. The bar should not be lowered in the examination guidelines for software.

For biotech patents, the requirements are still more stringent: in many cases, inventors must deposit a sample. The justification is that no paper

8. Kahin (1991).

description of a living organism is sufficient to allow anyone to make and use the organism, but the precedent is there for the USPTO to take the invention itself instead of its description.

There is an easy, concise way to deliver a program to the USPTO: provide the source code. Disk space is cheap—certainly cheaper than the storage of biomatter—so there is no logistic reason why source code cannot be filed with every software patent. The only problem is that the software companies want to reveal as little as possible to obtain a patent. If they could file the online manual as their claims, they would. But a patent is a contract between the public and the patent-holder: the public gives an individual a monopoly, and in return the individual provides the public with information that otherwise would have been kept secret. The courts and USPTO should ensure that software authors uphold their end of the bargain by revealing their innovative code.

### Make the Source Code Searchable

It is currently impossible for a programmer to know if the function he or she just wrote is patented. First, users must find just the right search term, which is an ordeal in itself—recall, for example, that Acacia's patent on streaming media over the Internet uses neither the terms "streaming media" nor "Internet." Programmers then need to read through pages of legalese to determine exactly what the patent covers. Then, they must repeat the process for every level of code: functions, data structures, libraries, on up to the user-level program.

If software is to remain covered by patents, programmers must be able to easily determine which routines are patented for which applications, and the process must be as quick as looking up a function's interface. The only alternative, which is current practice, is for programmers to forgo the patent search entirely, on the assumption that if they are in violation of anything significant a lawyer will contact them. This is clearly a suboptimal solution: in the economic sense, it creates risk and inefficiency, and in the technological sense, it does not permit practitioners to learn from relevant prior patents.

Independent invention is not a defense against infringement claims, and the software industry is massively decentralized. For true compliance, every computer user in the United States must legally clear every function or chain of operations that he or she writes down; this can only happen if searching the patent database is incredibly fast and cheap. Readers who find such a requirement onerous to the point of absurdity may prefer the alternative described in the next section.

## Eliminating Software Patents Altogether

In chapter 4, I proposed that an innovative state machine (a physical device) should have every right to a patent, while the states to which that machine are set (pure information) should not be patentable. This distinction meets the three criteria set out earlier, of allowing physical machines to be patented, ensuring that mathematics is not patented, and being clear and easy to apply. It also seems to be in line with the centuries of legal opinion prior to the rulings of the Court of Appeals for the Federal Circuit (CAFC). Drawing this line between the patentable and the unpatentable means eliminating patents on software.

Patents fail to recognize the unique, fundamental traits of software:

—Software is math, which is a natural part of the public domain. Algorithms for calculating cosines or multiplying matrices have been removed from the public domain via software patents. Restrictions on subject matter that impose variable names on mathematical algorithms are no solution to this fundamental problem.

—Software production is massively decentralized: people in the basement of almost every corporation in America write code. The informational assumptions underlying patents—that all patents are common knowledge and gaining that knowledge incurs moderate costs on only a few parties—are clearly false for software.

—A given program is equivalent to any other that executes the same mathematical algorithm. Hence a properly written software patent will be of immense breadth, which makes it almost certain that all new software will infringe existing patents. Because software is based on abstraction and generalization, the risk of overlapping with existing patented techniques will always exist regardless of the details of patenting rules.

—Independent invention is incredibly common in mathematics and in computer science. A patent on the implementation of a program protects the source code, just as a copyright would, but it would grant the first to patent the right to sue those who independently derive the algorithm, meaning that patent-holders need only wait and somebody prosecutable for damages will appear. Conversely, anyone who writes code is likely to independently derive a patented algorithm. Copyright protects the same text that a good patent would but without allowing the copyright-holder to sue independent inventors.

As well as fixing these fundamental problems, eliminating software patents would have a number of practical benefits:

—It would relieve the pressures on the USPTO, which is buried under a mountain of tens of thousands of software patent applications a year. As a result, software patents are underevaluated and funds diverted from the physical patent applications that the USPTO has shown success with in the past. Simply denying patents that are pure information would help defuse an impending funding disaster at the USPTO and provide a better quality of evaluation to physical patents.

—Legal ambiguities about whether any given mathematical algorithm is patented disappear, meaning fewer lawsuits and legal fees.

—Collaborative software can continue to exist without fear of being litigated out of existence.

—Consultants and information technology departments would be free to implement the best solution they know instead of being forced to purchase shrink-wrapped software with the appropriate legal coverage.

—Because writing software would be a less risky activity, more people would engage in it. Everyone who works in front of a computer—not just firms with research labs and a legal department—would be able to write innovative code.

—Anyone would be free to extend the value of a program by inventing interoperable products.

—Students of computer science would be free to learn from existing practitioners.

For all of these reasons, eliminating software patents may encourage innovation.

There is also abundant evidence that the software market would not collapse or stagnate without software patents. Before the decisive *In re Alappat* ruling in 1994, software patents were in legal limbo: nobody knew whether they would survive judicial scrutiny. Yet innovation and investment was closer to overheated than stagnant. Almost all of the tools of modern computing in common use—word processors, spreadsheets, databases, World Wide Web, e-mail—were all substantially in place in 1994. It is anyone's guess where drug manufacturing would be without patents, but not so for software: a software industry without software patents was alive and well from the 1950s up to a decade ago, and by any measure of innovation it was a resounding success.

The fundamental goal of patents is to ensure that innovators can sufficiently differentiate themselves from imitators. As discussed throughout this book, two pieces of software that implement the same basic algorithm can differ in many other ways. Two nontrivial programs will truly match only if one cut and pasted code from the other at some point in the development of the imitating program.

A patent on specific lines of code could protect against cutting and pasting, but such a regime is identical to a copyright—except that it allows patent-holders to sue anyone who independently implements the patented invention. This is an incredibly broad power that has been widely abused yet is unnecessary to protect the work an inventor has put into implementing a good program.

## Enforcing Copyright for Code

The only legal machinery needed to ensure such protection is a mechanism designed to evaluate the claim, "You copied my code." As *SCO* v. *IBM* shows, systematic rules for evaluating this claim are clearly inadequate at present, even though such assessment can be relatively easy, thanks to the reams of backups and version information that support a project.

If two programs look uncannily similar, the resemblance is not yet evidence that one plagiarized the other; conversely, if a programmer plagiarized a C program and implemented it in Perl, the two equivalent programs would not look at all alike. The existing abstraction-filtration-comparison test is hard to administer and is open to judicial interpretation. A process-oriented scheme, in which an arbitrator would ask whether the alleged infringer had copied code or rederived code, is easier to implement and interpret, given the reality of coding standards.

If people are to produce innovative or creative works, they need some assurance that competitors will not market photocopies of their work. In other words, to remain healthy, the software market needs an easy way to evaluate accusations of plagiarism. But authors do not need a lock on the market or a monopoly on an idea to viably design new code. Obviously, inventors will constantly clamor for such a gift from society, which they will claim to need and deserve, but experience has shown that this is too dear a cost. Although it is essential to protect the investment put into implementing an idea, society is better off when the idea itself is free to flourish in the minds and works of everyone.

# Glossary

**Assignee**   The patent applicant must be a human being or a group of humans. However, the inventors can assign the rights conferred by the patent to a company, usually the inventors' employer, to administer the patent, collect royalties, and so forth.

**Assembly language**   A one-to-one translation of *machine code*, wherein each instruction or memory address is given a human-readable mnemonic. A given processor can only understand one (or at best a handful of) assembly language(s), while one assembly language is specific to the handful of pieces of hardware that implement it.

**Best-mode rule**   A patent application must describe the best mode by which a program can be implemented, which prevents certain types of gaming of the system. This rule is basically ignored in practice, since it is so difficult to prove that a work is not in its best mode. I propose that a claim for a program implemented at the wrong level, without using available function libraries, or in an obfuscated manner should not pass this rule.

**Blocking patent**   A patent that can only function if used in conjunction with another patent. Neither patent-holder can implement the new innovation until both arrive at mutually agreeable terms.

**Breadth**   A term describing the variety of inventions that a patent or copyright covers. There are no accurate measures of the true breadth of a patent, but an examiner for a given patent has the power to modify the claim language to make it broader or narrower.

161

**CAFC**   Court of Appeals for the Federal Circuit. A court created in 1982 to hear primarily trade disputes and patent cases. Because the Supreme Court so rarely hears patent cases, the CAFC is more or less the highest court in the land for patent cases.

**Church-Turing thesis**   Any effective computation can be carried out by a *Turing machine*, and a Turing machine can carry out any effective computation. The word *effective* refers to any finite sequence of precise instructions. The hypothesis establishes an equivalence class: any program that is equivalent to a Turing machine will be equivalent to any other program that is equivalent to a Turing machine. This thesis answers the question "What problems are computable?" Alan Turing addressed the question in a 1936 paper describing the Turing machine, and in the same year Alonzo Church published his response based on the *lambda calculus*. The two were then shown to be equivalent.

**Circumvention device**   17 U.S.C. §1201(3)(a): "To 'circumvent a technological measure' means to descramble a scrambled work, to decrypt an encrypted work, or otherwise to avoid, bypass, remove, deactivate, or impair a technological measure, without the authority of the copyright owner."

**Clean room**   A group of programmers who can document that they have never looked closely at a competitor's code (although others in the same organization may have done so). Thus it can be documented that all code that comes out of the clean room has been independently invented, and so all such code runs zero risk of copyright infringement—but still bears the full risk of patent infringement. (Not to be confused with the software engineering method by the same name, which is aimed at producing bug-free code.)

**Compiler**   A program to translate code from a human-readable language to a computer's *machine code*. The user writes the source code, and then the compiler noninteractively produces a program. Compare with *interpreter*.

**Computable**   A problem that can be programmed on a *Turing machine* (and that the Turing machine can complete in finite time).

**Contributory infringement**   35 U.S.C. §271(a) states that selling or even simply using a device that is known to infringe a patent is itself an infringement of the patent.

**Copy protection**   17 U.S.C. §1201(3)(b): "A technological measure 'effectively controls access to a work' if the measure, in the ordinary course of its operation, requires the application of information, or a process or a treatment, with the authority of the copyright owner, to gain access to the work."

**Debugger**   A program that steps through every instruction of another program one by one. If the program being debugged includes a *symbol table*, then the instructions would be lines of human-readable code; if no symbol table is included, the instructions would be commands in *machine code*.

**DMCA**   Digital Millennium Copyright Act. This act outlawed the distribution of a *circumvention device* that gets around or breaks any sort of *copy protection*.

**Doctrine of equivalents**   If a device does not literally infringe the text of a patent but performs substantially the same function in substantially the same way to achieve substantially the same result, the device is still taken to be infringing. The doctrine is judicially created but has a history dating back to 1853 (to *Winans* v. *Denmead*, 56 U.S. [15 How] 330 [1853]).

**Enablement rule**   A patent must enable the reader to do something that he or she could not have done without the patent. This typically means that the invention must be described with sufficient detail to enable an appropriately skilled reader to implement the invention.

**Encryption**   The process of making data illegible by applying a series of transformations. If the transformations are reversed correctly, then the data can be read perfectly, but to one who does not know the correct transformations, the data are gibberish.

**Fair use**   The types of copying a copyrighted work that are considered acceptable uses, such as excerpting a passage from a novel in a review or making a backup copy of a CD.

**Free software**   See *open-source software*.

**FLOSS**   Free, Libre, and Open-Source Software. See *open-source software*.

**Function**   A list of instructions to a computer that takes a set of inputs and returns a set of known outputs. Modeled on mathematical functions such as $f(x) = x^2$, which some write as $f : x \to x^2$ to indicate that $f$ takes $x$ as an input and spits out $x^2$ as an output.

**Function library**   A set of functions and data structures used for a particular task. If the library has a function named `main`, the library is known as a program; if it does not, its functions may be called by other programs as needed.

**Incomplete appropriability**   The benefit of intellectual property protection: competitors cannot appropriate the whole of the original author's work as their own.

**Interpreter**   A program to translate code from a human-readable language to a computer's *machine code*. The user inputs individual commands, and then the interpreter produces the appropriate machine code and executes that code. Compare with *compiler*.

**Lambda calculus**   A notation for pure mathematical functions, so named because a function is expressed as a list of the form (λ in out). Programming languages that implement some variant of the lambda calculus include Lisp, Scheme, and Mathematica.

**Libre software**   See *open-source software*.

**Linux**   An operating system that complies with the POSIX standard. The first version was written by Linus Torvalds in his spare time, but he has since added contributions from hundreds of programmers. The *compiler*, shells, and other essential programs are often referred to as a part of Linux, but the name actually refers only to the kernel, which is the bridge between the other programs and the hardware.

**Machine language**   A language consisting of hexadecimal numbers that a computer chip can directly interpret as instructions. The machine language is the interface that the chip implements.

**Object code**   Code in *machine language*. It is specific to the few computers that can readily understand the machine language as a series of instructions. It is not human readable.

**Open-source software (OSS)**   Software whose source code is freely available, so users can modify or add to it. Most OSS licenses include a stipulation that users' changes or additions must also remain open source.

**Patent thicket**   A large bundle of patents, often all relating to one subfield, such that it is very difficult to write in this subfield without using some patents from the thicket. The metaphor refers to an inventor attempting to progress through the jungle, blocked at every turn by dense foliage.

**Port**   Rewriting code written for one set of libraries (such as those for MacOS) so that it will work on another (such as those for Windows). Sometimes also used to refer to rewriting code written in one language (such as C) in another (such as FORTRAN).

**POSIX**   The Portable Operating System Interface standard. By the mid-1980s, a multitude of variants on the UNIX operating system appeared; the Institute of Electrical and Electronics Engineers convened a panel to write this standard so that programs written on one flavor of UNIX could be more easily ported to another flavor. Santa Cruz Operation's UNIX, International Business Machines' AIX, Hewlett-Packard's HP-UX, Linux, and others all more or less comply with this standard.

**Prior art**   The existing published works that are searched to establish that a claim is novel. Theoretically, prior art includes all published works the world over, but since patent examiners are mortal, they often search only prior patents.

**Rent seeking**   Activity aimed at transferring money to one party from another. The receiving party is wealthier, but the society as a whole is no richer (although rent-seeking activity may be a small, unproductive part of an overall productive activity). If Company A could somehow extract $1 million from Company B by burning $900,000, it would be happy to do so, but the total value held by both companies would be down $900,000.

**Scène à faire**   Part of a creative work that "has to be done," such as methods of character development or plot devices in a story, or code that is required to conform to a standard.

**Shrink-wrapped software**   Software that is sold as a good, at a unit cost, and without customization.

**Source code**   The human-readable version of a program. It will be converted into *object code* for the computer to execute.

**State machine**   See *Turing machine*.

**Submarine patent**   A patent that is kept out of sight from other practitioners. Historically, this was achieved through bureaucratic wrangling with the USPTO to keep an application unpublished. Since there are so many software patents and the search problem is so much more difficult for them, it is reasonable to apply this term to a software patent that has been granted but not announced to the industry.

**Symbol table**   A table, produced by a *compiler* or *interpreter*, showing how each word in a program translates to machine code. For example, a variable such as todays_date may translate to the memory address 0xbffff590. Programmers may choose to leave the symbol table in the compiled object code (to facilitate debugging) or have the compiler discard the symbol table (which makes de-compiling by competitors difficult).

**Transistor**  A solid-state component with two inputs (the base and the emitter) and one output (the collector). If there is a current flowing through both the base and emitter, there will also be a current flowing through the collector. The transistor may thus be used to implement the logical AND.

**Trivial**  A technical term used by mathematicians to indicate that a problem can be solved using no creativity but perhaps great effort. Building an airplane given all the parts and complete instructions is trivial.

**Turing complete**  Describes a programming language that is equivalent to a *Turing machine*, in the sense of being equivalent to a set of states and instructions regarding a data tape. Any Turing complete language can be *trivially* translated into any other Turing complete language. The *lambda calculus* is Turing complete.

**Turing machine**  A theoretical device that is capable of a number of data-processing methods; a program specifies how the device switches between data-processing states. Also, any physical device that implements such a machine (such as a personal computer), or software that implements such a machine. Also known as a state machine.

**UNIX**  An operating system developed at Bell Labs. Many call any UNIX-like operating system by this name (often by the plural, Unices), but UNIX properly refers only to the code written by Bell Labs, which has evolved into code owned by Santa Cruz Operation. Others are correctly called POSIX-compliant. The name does not stand for anything, but is a pun on a predecessor operating system, Multics.

# References

Aharonian, Greg, and Richard Stim. 2004. "Patenting Art and Entertainment: New Strategies for Protecting Creative Ideas." Berkeley, Calif.: NOLO Press.

Allison, John R., and Mark A. Lemley. 2000. "How Federal Circuit Judges Vote in Patent Validity Cases." *Florida State University Law Review* 27 (Spring): 745–66.

Bakos, Yannis, and Erik Brynjolfsson. 1999. "Bundling Information Goods: Pricing, Profits, and Efficiency." *Management Science* 45 (December): 1613–30.

Battilana, Michael C. 1995. "The GIF Controversy: A Software Developer's Perspective." January 27; rev. June 20, 2004 (cloanto.com/users/mcb/19950127giflzw.html).

Bessen, James, and Robert M. Hunt. 2004a. "An Empirical Look at Software Patents." Research on Innovation Working Paper 03-17/R. Draft, March (www.researchoninnovation.org/swpat.pdf).

———. 2004b. "A Reply to Hahn and Wallsten." March 10, 2004 (www.researchoninnovation.org/hahn.pdf).

Bikhchandani, Sushil, David Hirshleifer, and Ivo Welch. 1992. "A Theory of Fads, Fashion, Custom, and Cultural Change as Informational Cascades." *Journal of Political Economy* 100 (51): 992–1026.

Brock, William A., and Steven N. Durlauf. 2001. "Discrete Choice with Social Interactions." *Review of Economic Studies* 68: 235–60.

Burk, Dan L., and Mark A. Lemley. 2002. "Is Patent Law Technology-Specific?" *Berkeley Tech. Law Journal* 17: 1155 (ssrn.com/abstract=349761).

Chen, Yongmin. 1997. "Equilibrium Product Bundling." *Journal of Business* 70 (January): 85–103.

Cherry, Steven M. 2004. "The Patent Profiteers." *IEEE Spectrum*, May 28, 2004 (www.spectrum.ieee.org/WEBONLY/publicfeature/jun04/0604aca.html).

Church, Alonzo. 1936a. "A Note on the Entscheidungsproblem." *Journal of Symbolic Logic* 1: 40–41.

———. 1936b. "An Unsolvable Problem of Elementary Number Theory." *American Journal of Mathematics* 58: 345–63.

Cifuentes, Cristina, and Anne Fitzgerald. 1999. "Is Reverse Engineering Always Legal?" Institute of Electrical and Electronics Engineers IT Pro, March/April, pp. 42–48.

Coase, Ronald H. 1960. "The Problem of Social Cost." *Journal of Law and Economics* 3: 1–23.

Cohen, Wesley M., Richard R. Nelson, and John P. Walsh. 2000. "Protecting Their Intellectual Assets: Appropriability Conditions and Why U.S. Manufacturing Firms Patent (or Not)." Working Paper 7552. Cambridge, Mass.: National Bureau of Economic Research (February).

Crouch, Dennis. 2004. "Eolas, Microsoft, and Pellegrini." *Patently Obvious*, October 14 (www.patentlyobviousblog.com/2004/10/eolas_microsoft.html).

Dam, Kenneth W. 1995. "Some Economic Considerations in the Intellectual Property Protection of Software." *Journal of Legal Studies* 24 (June): 321–77.

Davis, Martin. 2000. *The Universal Computer: The Road from Leibniz to Turing.* New York: W.W. Norton.

Federal Trade Commission (FTC). 2002. *Hearing on Competition and Intellectual Property Law and Policy in the Knowledge-Based Economy.* Washington, March 20 (www.ftc.gov/opp/intellect/020320trans.pdf).

———. 2003. *To Promote Innovation: The Proper Balance of Competition and Patent Law and Policy.* Washington, October (www.ftc.gov/os/2003/10/innovationrpt.pdf).

Gale, David, and Lloyd S. Shapley. 1962. "College Admissions and the Stability of Marriage." *American Mathematical Monthly* 69 (January): 9–15.

Galli, Peter. 2003. "Open Source on Rise in Government." *eWeek*, July 10 (www.eweek.com/article2/0,3959,1189729,00.asp).

Ghosh, Rishab Aiyer, Ruediger Glott, Bernhard Krieger, and Gregorio Robles. 2002. "FLOSS Developer Level Analysis." Working Paper. Heerlen, Netherlands: International Institute of Infonomics.

Gilbert, Richard J., and Michael L Katz. 2002. "An Economist's Guide to U.S. v. Microsoft." *Journal of Economic Perspectives* 15 (Spring): 25–44.

Hahn, Robert W., and Scott Jonathan Wallsten. 2003. "A Review of Bessen and Hunt's Analysis of Software Patents." November (ssrn.com/abstract=467484).

International Institute of Infonomics. 2004. "Free/Libre and Open Source Software: Survey and Study Final Report." Heerlen, Netherlands (www.infonomics.nl/FLOSS/).

Jaffe, Adam B., and Josh Lerner. 2004. *Innovation and Its Discontents: How Our Broken Patent System Is Endangering Innovation and Progress, and What to Do about It.* Princeton University Press.

Kahin, Brian. 1990. "The Software Patent Crisis." *Technology Review* (April): 543–58.

———. 1991. "The Case against 'Software Patents.'" *Optima: The Mathematical Programming Society Newsletter,* no. 33 (June).

Klemens, Ben. 2003. "Information Aggregation, with Application to Monotone Ordering, Conviviality, and Advocacy." Ph.D. dissertation, California Institute of Technology (fluff.info/klemens/klemens_ diss.pdf).

Klemperer, Paul. 1990. "How Broad Should the Scope of Patent Protection Be?" *RAND Journal of Economics* 21 (Spring): 113–30.

Knight, Andrew F. 2004. "A Potentially New IP: Storyline Patents." *Journal of the Patent and Trademark Office Society* 86 (November).

Krim, Jonathan. 2003. "Patenting Air or Protecting Property? Information Age Invents a New Problem." *Washington Post,* December 11 (www.washingtonpost.com/ac2/wp-dyn/A54548-2003Dec10).

Landes, William M., and Richard A. Posner. 2003. *The Economic Structure of Intellectual Property Law.* Cambridge, Mass.: Belknap Press.

Lessig, Lawrence. 1999. *Code and Other Laws of Cyberspace.* New York: Basic Books.

Mann, Ronald. 2004. "The Myth of the Software Patent Thicket: An Empirical Investigation of the Relationship between Intellectual Property and Innovation in Software Firms." Law and Economics Working Paper 022. Austin: University of Texas School of Law (February).

Merges, Robert P., Peter S. Menell, and Mark A. Lemley. 2000. *Intellectual Property in the New Technological Age.* New York: Aspen Law and Business.

Merrill, Stephen A., Richard C. Levin, and Mark B. Meyers, eds. 2004. *A Patent System for the 21st Century.* Washington: National Academies Press.

Moore, Carmella C., A. Kimball Romney, and Ti-Lien Hsia. 2002. "Cultural, Gender, and Individual Differences in Perceptual and Semantic Structures of Basic Colors in Chinese and English." *Journal of Cognition and Culture* 2 (1): 1–28.

National Research Council. 2002. *The Digital Dilemma: Intellectual Property in the Information Age.* Washington: National Academies Press.

Niskanen, William A. 1971. *Bureacruacy and Representative Government.* Hawthorne, N.Y.: Aldine Atherton.

Olson, Mancur. 1971. *Logic of Collective Action: Public Goods and the Theory of Groups.* Harvard University Press.

Palfrey, Thomas R. 1983. "Bundling Decisions by a Multiproduct Monopolist with Incomplete Information." *Econometrica* 51 (March): 463–84.

Poole, Keith T., and Howard Rosenthal. 1985. "A Spatial Model for Legislative Roll Call Analysis." *American Journal of Political Science* 29 (May): 357–84.

Rai, Arti Kaur. 2002. "Facts, Law, and Policy: An Allocation-of-Powers Approach to Patent System Reform." Law and Economics Research Paper 02-20. University of Pennsylvania Institute for Law and Economics, October (ssrn.com/abstract=335122).

Schoen, Lawrence, and Klingon Language Institute. 2000. *The Klingon Hamlet.* New York: Pocket Books.

Trajtenberg, Manuel. 1990. "A Penny for Your Quotes: Patent Citations and the Value of Innovations." *RAND Journal of Economics* 21 (1990): 172–87.

Turing, Alan M. 1936–37. "On Computable Numbers, with an Application to the Entscheidungsproblem." *Proceedings of the London Mathematical Society*, ser. 2 (42): 230–65.

U.S. Patent and Trademark Office (USPTO). 2004. *Manual of Patent Examining Procedure*, 8th ed. Washington: Government Printing Office (May).

Welch, T. A. 1984. "A Technique for High-Performance Data Compression." *IEEE Computer* 17 (6): 8–19.

Williams, Sam. 2002. *Free as in Freedom: Richard Stallman's Crusade for Free Software.* Cambridge, Mass.: O'Reilly Press.

# Index

Abstraction-filtration-comparison (AFC) test. *See* Courts and judicial systems

Acacia Technologies, 5, 89–90

Adobe Systems, 6, 77–78, 97–98, 103, 127

AFC test (abstraction-filtration-comparison test). *See* Courts and judicial systems

Agulnik, David, 20–21

Aharonian, Greg, 60

Algorithms. *See* Mathematics

Amazon.com, 6, 99

American Airlines, 94

American Enterprise Institute–Brookings Joint Center for Regulatory Studies, 74

American Video Graphics, 6

Antitrust issues, 110, 111

Apache, 95, 99–100

Apple Computer, Inc., 6, 18, 104, 109

*Art of Programming* (Knuth), 118

Assembly language. *See* Computer coding and programming—specific languages

AT&T, 143, 145

Bell Labs, 33, 143

Berkeley Internet Name Daemon (BIND), 95, 99

Bernstein, Daniel, 122

*Bernstein v. U.S. Department of State, et al. (1997)*, 121–22

Bessen, James, 74

Binary Large Object (BLOB). *See* Files and formats—specific

Binary numbers. *See* Computer coding and programming; Mathematics

BIND. *See* Berkeley Internet Name Daemon

Black, Edward J., 87

BLOB (Binary Large Object). *See* Files and formats—specific

*Bowers v. Baystate Technologies (2003)*, 139

British Technology Group, 6

Brotz, Douglas, 77

Browne, Lee, 78

Brown, James Cooke, 117

Bureau of Economic Analysis, 92

Burk, Dan, 133

Cabbage Patch Kids, 14, 142

CADAM, Inc., 94

CAFC. *See* Court of Appeals for the Federal Circuit

Calculators. *See* Computer coding and programming; Computers

Camino browser. *See* Software and software programs—specific

Carroll, Lewis, 121

*Chamberlain Group, Inc.* v. *Skylink Techs, Inc.* (2004), 128

Chambers, John, 118

Church, Alonzo, 26, 29, 35

Church-Turing thesis, 26, 35, 47, 50, 58, 63

Circuit boards. *See* Computers

Cisco Systems, 103

Coase's theorem, 48, 81, 102

Coca-Cola Company, 136

Cohen, Wesley, 81–82

Compilers. *See* Software and software programs—specific

Computer and Communications Industry Association, 87

*Computer Associates International* v. *Altai* (1992), 147, 149

Computer coding and programming: algorithms and, 25, 26; arrays, 37; binary code or notation, 25, 28, 31–32, 53–54; choice and use of languages, 34–35; collaborative programming, 94–96, 98, 105, 106; data structures and functions of, 25, 26, 27–29, 36–38, 40–43, 101, 109, 115, 116, 121, 140, 146; debugging, 137–39; decentralized programming, 100–03; field-programmable gate arrays, 65–68; file formats and, 38, 115; hiding of implementation, 41–42; instructions and rules, 29–31, 33, 34, 36–37; interfaces and implementation, 26–27; libraries, 41, 42, 61, 81, 100, 101, 109–14, 116, 118, 133–34, 145–46; mathematics and,

26, 51; porting and translating, 145–46; programming languages and translation, 25, 26, 32, 33–34, 35, 43, 50, 116, 118, 119, 146; protection of, 118–19; in the public domain, 135–36; reading and writing code, 140; registers, 28, 29, 30–31, 32, 33, 40, 137; summary of, 24–27; symbol tables, 32f, 33, 35–36, 42–43, 137–38; as a trade secret, 137–41; triviality of, 25, 26, 35, 40, 41, 43, 50, 64, 66, 67; Turing completeness of, 35–36; versions of, 148–49. *See also* Copyright; Glossary; Logic; Patents; Policy recommendations; Software and software programs

Computer coding and programming—examples: assembly-language symbol table, 32, 33; deCSS code, 126; find_person, 40, 41; pop-up window, 2; reading Word documents, 39; signal code, 144; tab-browsing, 22; translation of code, 146

Computer coding and programming—specific languages: assembly or machine code, 31, 33–34, 41–42, 65, 134; C, 33–34, 35–36, 42–43, 134, 144, 145; FORTRAN, 43, 146; Java, 6–7, 66, 67, 86, 96, 110–11; JavaScript, 2, 134; Mono, 119, 120–21; .NET, 119, 120–21; Perl, 16, 35–36, 118; S, 118; TEX, 118; VisualBasic, 42–43; XML (extensible markup language), 37–38, 116n11, 129. *See also* Glossary

Computers: AND, OR, and NOT gates, 27, 30; building and design of, 30–31, 32; calculators, 29; chips and chip manufacture, 31, 64, 65; circuits and circuit boards, 25, 28, 29; downloading to, 138; execution of instructions, 34; field-programmable gate arrays, 64, 65–68; future of, 104;

hard discs or drives, 37, 57–59, 115; line between hardware and software, 64–68; memory addresses, 33, 34; patents and, 31, 32, 57–58, 82–83, 153; processors of, 25, 40; programming languages and, 32, 34; semiconductors of, 27; states and state machines and, 25, 29–30, 45–46, 62, 64–65, 66, 67–68, 153; transistors in, 27–28, 31. *See also* Logic; Software and software programs

Congress (U.S.), 51–53, 68–69, 71, 72, 152, 152–54

Content Scrambling Scheme (CSS and deCSS), 123–24

Copyright: abstraction-filtration-comparison test and, 147, 149; allowable subjects, 146; basics of, 14–15; breadth of, 141–42; collaborative software and, 98; copying and, 130; of computer programming languages, 116, 119–20, 121; disassembly and, 139; DMCA and, 123, 127, 130; duration of, 142; economic issues, 15–16, 17, 121, 141–42; fair use and, 138; function of, 14; of ideas, 117, 119–20, 142, 148–49; of implementation, 143–49; independent authorship and invention, 8, 124, 131–32, 142; infringement of, 15, 123–24, 131–32, 139, 141–42, 146–47; of interfaces, 116–21, 141–42; mathematical exception in, 146; plagiarism, 8, 14, 137, 139, 141, 142–44, 145, 147–49; of software, 16, 103, 138, 140–41; of source code, 116, 119–20, 131, 137–49, 158–60. *See also* Glossary

Copyright—specific, 14, 15, 121

Court of Appeals for the Federal Circuit (CAFC): cases of, 56–60, 69–70, 78, 128; as a pro-patent court, 45, 70, 71–72; view of mathematics and software, 53, 63, 68–69, 133, 158

Court of Appeals for the Federal Circuit—specific cases: *Bowers* v. *Baystate Technologies* (2003), 139; *Chamberlain Group, Inc.* v. *Skylink Techs, Inc.* (2004), 128; *Information International Incorporated* v. *Adobe, et al.*, 78; *In re Alappat* (1994), 45, 57–58, 62, 66, 155, 159; *In re Lowry* (1994), 115; *State Street Bank & Trust* v. *Signature Financial Group* (1998), 45, 58–60, 62, 66, 75, 155

Court of Customs and Patent Appeals, 55

Courts and judicial systems: abstraction-filtration-comparison test, 131, 142n13, 148, 149, 159–60; copyright infringement cases, 15; determination of patentability, 44–45, 47, 48; interpretation of Patent Acts, 51–52; patent infringement cases, 13, 69; regulatory capture and, 70–71; reversal of USPTO errors and, 77; *scène à faire* rule, 144–45; software patentability, 52, 69–70. *See also* Court of Appeals for the Federal Circuit; Supreme Court

Creative Labs, 6

CSS. *See* Content Scrambling Scheme

Dam, Kenneth, 3

Defense, Department of, 105

Dell Computer Corporation, 6

DE Technologies, 6

Diamond Rio, 18

*Diamond* v. *Chakrabarty* (1980), 59

*Diamond* v. *Diehr* (1981), 8, 44–45, 55–56, 57, 69n32

Diehr, James, 55

Digital Millennium Copyright Act (DMCA; 1998), 1, 108, 109, 115, 121–30, 139

Digital processors, 25

Digital Versatile Disc Copy Control Association (DVD CCA), 123–24, 125

Digital versatile discs. *See* DVDs

District Court of the Eastern District of Kentucky, 128

District Court of the Sixth Circuit, 128

DMCA. *See* Digital Millennium Copyright Act

Dudas, John W., 70–71

DVD CCA. *See* Digital Versatile Disc Copy Control Association

DVDs (digital versatile discs), 123–25, 130

*Eastman Kodak* v. *Sun Microsystems* (2004), 6–7, 86

eBooks. *See* Electronic books

Economic issues: competition, 112, 113, 116, 128–29, 149; copyrights, 15–16, 17; costs, 96–97, 102; DMCA, 130; implementation versus interface, 116; innovation, 74; lock-in problems, 112; markets, 17, 112; monopolies and monopolists, 112, 151, 152, 156; patents, 3, 5, 14, 15, 16–23, 47–48, 76, 132, 151–52; prices, 96, 112–14; property rights, 81; rent seeking, 82; software, 3–4, 9, 10, 92–93, 96–100; standards, 115

Eharmony.com, 61, 63

Electronic books (eBooks), 127

Electronic Frontier Foundation, 99

Electronics and electronic components, 28–29, 51–52. *See also* Computers

Eli Lilly, 18. *See also* Prozac

Encryption, 121–30

End-user license agreement (EULA), 139

Enigma code, 122

Eolas, 6, 86–87

*Eolas Technologies* v. *Microsoft* (2003), 86

EU. *See* European Union

EULA. *See* End-user license agreement

European Commission, 96

European Patent Office, 9

European Union (EU), 9, 95, 103, 139

Extensible markup language (XML). *See* Computer coding and programming—specific languages

Federal–Mogul Corporation, 55

Federal Trade Commission (FTC), 76–77, 133, 151, 152

Feist Publications, 147

Field-programmable gate arrays (FPGAs). *See* Computers

Files and formats, 38, 115–16

Files and formats—specific: Binary Large Object (BLOB), 94, 129; DOC, 38, 115, 129; eBook, 127; PDF, 35, 127; Windows Media Audio (WMA), 129

Firefox browser. *See* Software and software programs—specific

Firewire. *See* IEEE *1394* standard

First Amendment issues, 122, 124, 125

FLOSS (Free, Libre, and Open-Source Software), 95

Flowcharts, 21–23, 43, 50–51, 59, 78, 131, 133

FPGAs (field-programmable gate arrays). *See* Computers

Fraunhofer Institute for Integrated Circuits, 89

Free, Libre, and Open-Source Software. *See* FLOSS

Free-Walter-Abele test, 56

FTC. *See* Federal Trade Commission

Gable, R. Lewis, 79

Gale, David, 48–49, 50–51, 59–60, 63

Garage door openers, 128

Garbage Pail Kids, 14, 142

Gates, Bill, 84, 111. *See also* Microsoft Corporation

Germany, 95, 122

GIF. *See* Graphics Interchange Format

GNU (GNU's Not Unix), 98

GNU Public License (GPL), 98

GNU Scientific Library (GSL), 61, 99

GNU's Not Unix. *See* GNU
Google, 6, 106
*Gottschalk* v. *Benson* (1972), 44, 53–54, 55, 59, 69, 77, 134, 154, 155
GPL. *See* GNU Public License
Graphics Interchange Format (GIF), 88
Gravity, 56
GSL. *See* GNU Scientific Library

Hahn, Robert, 74
Hardware, 63–68. *See also* Computers
Hunt, Robert M., 74

IBM (International Business Machines), 6, 84–85, 86, 96, 97, 103, 143
Ideaflood, Inc., 2
Ideas. *See* Copyright; Intellectual property; Patents
Id Software, 6
IE (Internet Explorer). *See* Software and software programs—specific
IEEE. *See* Institute of Electrical and Electronics Engineers
IEEE *1394* standard (Firewire), 115
IIS, 99–100
*Information International Incorporated* v. *Adobe, et al.*, 78
*In re Alappat* (1994), 45, 57–58, 62, 65, 69, 100n17, 155, 159
*In re Lowry* (1994), 57–58, 69, 115
Institute of Electrical and Electronics Engineers (IEEE), 144
Intellectual property (IP): copyright versus patent, 137; interoperability and, 108–14; legal issues, 108–11, 130; protection of, 1, 16–23, 46–47, 53, 103, 112–13, 114, 125, 129, 130; software intellectual property, 42, 43; trade–related intellectual property, 9. *See also* Copyright; Digital Millennium Copyright Act; Patent law issues; Patents
Intellectual Property Owners Association (IPO), 151–52

International Business Machines. *See* IBM
International Obfuscated C Code contest, 118
International Standards Organization (ISO), 88
Internet, 89–90, 94, 129
Internet Explorer (IE). *See* Software and software programs—specific
Interoperability, 108. *See also* Software and software programs
Inventions and inventors, 51, 130, 136, 155, 160
IP. *See* Intellectual property
IPO. *See* Intellectual Property Owners Association
iPod, 18
ISO. *See* International Standards Organization

"Jabberwocky" (Carroll), 121
Jaffe, Adam, 71, 75
Java. *See* Computer coding and programming—specific languages
JavaScript. *See* Computer coding and programming—specific languages
Jefferson, Thomas, 20, 46–47, 51, 62, 155
Johansen, Jon Lech, 123, 124
*J2 Global Communications* v. *Mijanda, Inc.*, 100
Judicial and court systems. *See* Courts and judicial systems
Justice, Department of, 110

Kahin, Brian, 156
Kernighan, Brian, 143
Klingon, 117–18
Klingon Language Institute, 117
Knight, Andrew F., 60
Knuth, Donald, 118
Kodak. *See* Eastman Kodak v. Sun Microsystems

Language, 32n8, 117–18. *See also* Computer coding and programming

Lempel, Abraham, 88

Lerner, Josh, 71, 75

Lessig, Lawrence, 152

*Lexmark International* v. *Static Control Components* (2003), 127–28, 145

Libraries. *See* Computer coding and programming

Lilly. *See* Eli Lilly

Links browser. *See* Software and software programs—specific

Linux. *See* Operating systems

Lloyd's of London, 97

Lockheed, 94

Logic: binary notation and, 28; debuggers and, 137; design of computers and, 31, 32; electrical equivalents and, 27, 28; field-programmable gate arrays and, 65; gates and circuits, 28–29; implementation of, 29. *See also* Computer coding and programming; Computers; Mathematics; Software and software programs

Loglan, 117, 118, 119

Lojban, 117, 118, 119

Lutton, Theodore, 55

Lynx browser. *See* Software and software programs—specific

LZW algorithm, 88

Machine code. *See* Computer coding and programming—specific languages

*Mackay Radio & Telegraph Co.* v. *Radio Corp. of America* (1939), 146

MacOS. *See* Operating systems

Macromedia, 6, 97–98

Mann, Ronald, 5, 81, 84, 86, 140–41

*Manual of Patent Examining Procedure* (MPEP), 58, 75, 90

Massachusetts, 106

Mathematics: binary numbers, 25, 28, 31–32, 53–54; combinatorial optimization, 49; computer coding and, 26, 28, 31, 42–43; definition of, 51; factor analysis, 61; lambda calculus, 26, 35–36, 42–43, 50; language of, 32; ownership of results and algorithms, viii, ix, 6; patentability of, 4, 44–51, 53, 54, 55–56, 62; principal component analysis, 61. *See also* Software and software programs

Mathematics—algorithms and equations: independent invention and, 26; mathematical utility of, 48–51; patentability of, 45, 53–54, 56, 59–60, 63–64, 66, 69, 72, 154, 155; patent claims and, 131, 134, 136; publishing of, 130; software programs and, 42–43, 57

Mathematics—specific problems: marriage algorithm, 48–49, 50; Pythagorean Theorem, 54; singular value decomposition, 61; traveling salesman problem, 49, 49–50

Meredith Corporation, 147

Microsoft Corporation: antitrust action against, 110–11; libraries of, 109–10; patent infringement and, vii, viii, 6, 86, 99–100; patents of, 21–23, 38, 103, 115–16; standards and interoperability and, 109. *See also Eolas* v. *Microsoft*; Gates, Bill; Operating systems; Software and software programs—specific

Microsoft Excel. *See* Software and software programs—specific

Microsoft Word. *See* Software and software programs—specific

Molloy, Bryan, 2, 3

Morse, Samuel F. B., 51–52

*Moscow on the Hudson* (film), 15

Motion Picture Association of America (MPAA), 125

Motion Picture Experts Group, 88

Mozilla browser. *See* Software and software programs—specific

MPAA. *See* Motion Picture Association of America

*MPAA v. 2600 Magazine* (2000), 123–25

MPEG-I standard, 88–89

MPEP. *See Manual of Patent Examining Procedure*

MP3.com, 96

MP3s and MP3 players, 18, 88–89

Munich (Germany), 7

Music and movie industries, 10

National Academy of Sciences, 71, 72

National Research Council (NRC), 155

Nelson, Richard, 81–82

.NET. *See* Computer coding and programming—specific languages

Netscape, Inc., 110

Netscape Navigator. *See* Software and software programs—specific

Newspring, 19

Newton, Isaac, 24

*New Yorker* magazine, 15

*Northern Telecom* v. *Datapoint*, 133

Novell, Inc., 111, 143

*Novell v. Microsoft* (2001), 111

NRC. *See* National Research Council

Open-source projects. *See* Software and software programs

Opera browser. *See* Software and software programs—specific

Operating systems, 144

Operating systems—specific: Linux, vii–viii, 7, 100, 101, 123, 143–44; MacOS, 109, 110; UNIX, 96, 118, 143–44; Windows, vii, 99–100, 106, 109–10, 119. *See also* Glossary

Outsourcing and offshoring, 106

Ownership concepts, viii–ix

Palfrey, Tom, 112

Paramount Pictures, 118

*Parker* v. *Flook* (1978), 44, 54, 55, 59, 68

Patent Acts (*1793, 1836, 1870, 1874, 1952*), 51–53, 146

*Patenting Art and Entertainment: New Strategies for Protecting Creative Ideas* (Aharonian and Stim), 60

Patent law issues: economic factors, 97; Freeman-Walter-Abele test, 56; the future of software and, 107; independent invention, 47, 102, 157; mathematics, 51–60; patentable inventions, 51 ; infringement, 5–6, 13–14, 22–23, 38, 47, 79, 81, 83–90, 100n17, 131, 136, 157; suits, 13, 85–86, 90–91, 97–98, 100, 107

Patents: basics of, 12–14, 132, 135; best-mode rule, 135; blocking patents and compound inventions, 80–81, 82–85; breadth of, 16, 17–19, 68, 77, 78–79, 80–90, 108, 120, 136; collaborative software and, 98–99; of complex industries, 81–85; of computer programming languages, 120; computers and, 57–58; costs and benefits of, 5, 17–23, 102; coverage of, 8, 13, 18–19, 22–23; decentralization and, 101; descriptions and claims of, 4, 13, 135; doctrine of equivalents, 136; duration of, 2n2, 13, 132; enablement requirement, 132–33; general functions of, 12, 17, 85, 88, 91, 132, 159–60; GNU General Public License and, 98; guidelines for good patents, 18, 21, 23, 68, 135; of ideas, 47, 117, 120n16, 155–56; independent invention, 131; instability of, 90–91; on interfaces, 112, 114, 115–16; interoperability and, 115; licensing and, 80–81, 82, 84–85, 86, 116n10; for mathematics, 51–60, 146; motives for, 82–83; open source and, 97–100; patent searches and reviews, 13, 74–76, 79–80, 87, 91, 102, 155, 157; patent thickets, 83–85, 100, 101–02; prior art and, 75, 98–99, 154–55;

process of, 74–75; rejected and overturned patents, 75–76, 155; requirements of, 13n2, 44–45, 49; software
markets and, 103–04, 107; of source
code, 32, 37, 38–40, 43–44, 131–37;
state of patents today, 62–68; submarine patents, 16, 87–90, 91; viewing
and obtaining copies of, 2n2. *See also*
Courts and judicial systems;
Economic issues; Glossary; Policy recommendations; Software and software programs—patents and
patentability; *individual courts*
Patents—specific devices and programs:
Amazon's one-click purchasing, 99;
audio and video transmission system,
78–79, 89; banana protective
devices, 20–21; business methods,
59–60, 69; computer chips, 31;
Eharmony.com, 61; field-programmable gate arrays, 65–68; GIFs, 88;
hard drives, 57–59, 115; Java metadata interfaces, 66; Microsoft Word,
38–39; morse code and telegraph,
51–52; MP3s and MP3 players,
17–18, 88–89; online bill paying,
122; pop-up browser windows, 1, 2,
80; Prozac, 2, 3, 18–19; rubber-
curing and -molding machine, 44–45,
55; singular value decomposition
(SVD), 61, 102; streaming media, 89;
tabbed browsing, 21–23, 78, 80;
XML reading, 37–38, 78
Patents—specific numbers: *1,647*,
51–52; *4,314,081*, 2; *4,558,302*, 88;
*5,132,992*, 78, 89; *5,484,378*, 50;
*5,579,430*, 89; *5,742,735*, 89;
*5,835,392*, 63; *5,886,908*, 63;
*5,933,841*, 86; *5,960,422*, 99;
*5,974,686*, 19; *6,035,769*, 19;
*6,055,556*, 63; *6,056,138*, 19;
*6,078,938*, 63; *6,196,404*, 19;
*6,289,319*, 122; *6,356,926*, 63;
*6,389,458*, 1–2; *6,434,582*, 63;

*6,442,574*, 86; *6,612,440*, 20;
*6,640,237*, 63; *6,665,697*, 63;
*6,735,568*, 61; *6,745,215*, 63;
*6,785,865*, 21–23; *6,792,569*, 63;
*6,807,536*, 63; *6,905,665*, 50;
*6,918,122*, 66, 67
PDF (Portable Document Format). *See*
Files and file formats—specific
Perl programming language. *See*
Computer coding and programming—specific languages
Plagiarism. *See* Copyright
Policy recommendations: Congress and,
152–53; economic issues, 151–52;
elimination of software patents,
158–60; interface versus implementation, 156; mathematical issues,
155–56; software patents, 153–56;
source code issues, 156–58
Political issues: intellectual property pro-
tection, 8–9; patentability, 51–53;
regulatory capture, 70–71; software
and collective action, 102–03
Portable Document Format (PDF). *See*
Computer coding and program-
ming—specific languages
POSIX (Portable Operating System
Interface). *See* Standards
Private sector, 95
Programming. *See* Computer coding and
programming; Software and software
programs
Property rights, viii–ix, 81. *See also*
Intellectual property
Prozac, 2–3, 4, 18–19
Publications International, 146–47
Public domain, 2, 135–36, 158
Public sector, 95

Qualcomm Incorporated, 94

Rai, Arti Kaur, 72
Reback, Gary L., 84–85
Red Hat, 96

Reiser, Hans, 96
Remote controls, 128
Reverse engineering, 138–41
Rich, Giles, 58
Rio player, 18
Ritchie, Dennis, 143
Rubbermaid, 19
Rural Telephone Service, 147

SABRE Holdings, 94
Sachan/Eiger Labs, 18
Safari browser, 23
Santa Cruz Operation (SCO), 143
SAP, 84
Schmiegel, Klaus, 2, 3
Schwartz, Jonathan, 64
SCO. *See* Santa Cruz Operation
*SCO* v. *IBM (2003)*, 143–44, 160
*Sega Enterprises, Ltd.* v. *Accolade, Inc.*
   *(1992)*, 139
Selective serotonin reuptake inhibitor
   (SSRI), 4. *See also* Prozac
Semiconductors. *See* Computers
Shapley, Lloyd S., 48–49, 50–51, 59–60,
   63
Shuster, Brian, 1–2, 134
Singular value decomposition (SVD), 61,
   102
Sklyarov, Dmitri, 127
Skylink Techs, Inc., 128
Social contract, 132–37
Software and software programs: as
   complex products, 82; decentralized
   production, 100–03; downloading
   and running of, 13; economic issues,
   3–4, 9, 96–97; fair use of, 10, 138;
   free and open-source software, 6–7,
   94–100, 101, 103, 104, 105–06,
   107, 116n11; as function libraries,
   41, 42; future of, 104–07; hardware
   and, 63–68; implementation of,
   26–27, 116, 131, 156; in-house programming, 93–96; interfaces, 26–27,
   112, 114, 115–17, 156; interoper-

ability, 108–14, 115, 125–26; markets of, 10, 92–93, 100–04, 106–07;
   mathematics of, 4, 10, 49–51, 158;
   pricing of, 92–93; prior art, 23; protection of, 1, 21–23; text of source
   code, 131–49; tracking versions of,
   148–49; writing of, 5, 34–35. *See
   also* Copyright; Computer coding
   and programming; Computers;
   Intellectual property
Software and software programs—
   patents and patentability: breadth of,
   68, 73, 80, 136, 158; computers and,
   57, 153; courts and, 53–60, 69–72;
   disclosure requirements for, 133,
   134; elimination of patents, 158–60;
   equations and, 59–60; example of,
   21–23; filing source code, 132–37;
   hard discs and, 57–58; hold-up problem of, 85–87; innovation and invention and, 73–74, 77–78, 87, 158–59;
   legal aspects of, 62, 80; line between
   hardware and software, 44–45,
   64–68; mathematics and, 47, 50–51;
   obfuscation and, 133–35; patent
   length of, 16; patent thickets, 83–85;
   policy recommendations, 153–60;
   problems of patenting, 1–6, 74–80;
   submarine patents, 87–90
Software and software programs—specific: Adobe Acrobat, 127; Apache,
   95, 99–100; Berkeley Internet Name
   Daemon (BIND), 95, 99; business
   software, 105; Camino browser, 23;
   cdrecord, 130; compilers and inter-
   preters, 33–34, 41–42, 65, 137; concurrent versioning system, 148;
   debuggers, 137–38; disassemblers,
   138; doxygen, 140; Eharmony.com,
   61; e-mail, 95; encryption and
   decryption software, 122; field-programmable gate arrays, 65–68;
   Firefox browser, 23; games, 105;
   GAMS mathematical modeling soft-

ware, 94; ghostview, 127; Internet Explorer, 86, 99, 110; Links browser, 23; Lynx browser, 23; Microsoft Excel, 145; Microsoft Word, 35, 38–39, 42, 115–16, 119; Mozilla browser, 23; navigation of hyperlinks via tabs, 21–23; Netscape Navigator, 110, 122; OpenOffice.org, 105, 116; Opera browser, 23; pop-up browser windows, 1–2, 4; Postfix, 95; SABRE flight reservation system, 94; Sendmail, 95; spreadsheets, 41, 105, 145; StarOffice, 35, 116; subversion, 148; virus protection, 6; WordPerfect, 111, 116; word processors, 25, 37–38, 41, 105, 106, 116, 118–19; xine D5D, 130. *See also* Computer coding and programming—specific languages; Files and formats—specific; Glossary; Operating systems

Southwestern Bell Corporation, 86

Spaceships, 51

SSRI. *See* Selective serotonin reuptake inhibitor

Standards: creation of, 114–15; de facto standards, 108, 109–14; file formats, 115; MPEG-I standard, 88–89; Microsoft and, 109; Portable Operating System Interface (POSIX), 144, 145; USB standards, 114

Stanford University, 84–85

StarOffice. *See* Software and software programs—specific

*Star Trek* (TV), 117

State machines. *See* Computers

*State Street Bank & Trust* v. *Signature Financial Group* (1998), 45, 58–60, 62, 66, 72, 75, 155

Static Control Components, 127–28, 145

Steinberg, Saul, 15

Stim, Richard, 60

Sun Microsystems Inc.: IBM and, 84–85; Java, 6–7, 66, 67, 86, 96,

110; Kodak and, 86; libraries of, 110; open-source authors and, 97; patents of, 66, 67; president and CEO of, 64; word processor of, 35

Supreme Court: appeals of patent cases in, 13, 69; differences between state machines and states, 53; patent protection for software and, 8, 53–56, 128; telecommunications, 52

Supreme Court—specific cases: *Diamond* v. *Chakrabarty* (1980), 59; *Diamond* v. *Diehr* (1981), 8, 44–45, 55–56, 57, 69n32; *Gottschalk* v. *Benson* (1972), 44, 53–54, 55, 59, 69, 77, 134, 154, 155; *Mackay Radio & Telegraph Co.* v. *Radio Corp. of America* (1939), 146; *Parker* v. *Flook* (1978), 44, 54, 55

SVD. *See* Singular value decomposition

"Sweat of the brow protection," 150n22

Sweden, 95

Terrorism, 99, 122, 130

*1394 Trade Association*, 115

Toomey, Warren, 145

Topps baseball cards, 14

Torvalds, Linus, 144–45

Trademarks, 114, 115

Trade-related intellectual property (TRIP). *See* Intellectual property

Trade secrets, 124, 136, 137–41

Tupperware, 19

Turing, Alan, 26, 29, 30, 122

Turing machine, 29–30, 35, 102. *See also* Glossary

*2600 Magazine: The Hacker Quarterly*, 124–25

Unisys, 7, 88

United Kingdom (UK), 95, 122

United States (U.S.), 7, 122

*United States* v. *Microsoft* (2001), 110, 111n5

Universal serial bus (USB), 114

University of Illinois, 94

UNIX. *See* Operating systems

UNIX Heritage Society, 145

UNIX Systems Lab (USL), 143

USB. *See* Universal serial bus

USB Implementer's Forum, Inc. (USB-IF), 114, 115

USB.org, 114

USL. *See* UNIX Systems Lab

U.S. Patent and Trademark Office (USPTO): algorithms and, 56, 62–63; examiners and review process, 13, 74–80, 132, 154; funding for, 70–71, 159; monopolies and, 151; overload of, 74–75, 159; role and rulings of, 99, 154; software and, 2, 4, 5–6, 45, 74–75, 159; submarine patents and, 16. *See also* Patents

U.S. Supreme Court. *See* Supreme Court

USPTO. *See* U.S. Patent and Trademark Office

Vacuum tubes, 27, 28

Wall, Larry, 118

Wallsten, Scott, 74

Walsh, John, 81–82

Wang Laboratories, 7

Webbink, Mark, 87

Welch, Terry, 88

Windows. *See* Operating systems

Windows Media Audio (WMA). *See* Files and formats—specific

WordPerfect. *See* Software and software programs—specific

World Bank, 94

World War II, 122

XML (Extensible markup language). *See* Computer coding and programming—specific languages

Yahoo!, 6

Yurt, Paul, 78

Ziv, Jacob, 88